# 网球竞赛规则
# （2023）

中国网球协会　审定

人民体育出版社

图书在版编目（CIP）数据

网球竞赛规则. 2023 / 中国网球协会审定. -- 北京:
人民体育出版社, 2023 (2025.11重印)
ISBN 978-7-5009-6350-9

Ⅰ. ①网… Ⅱ. ①中… Ⅲ. ①网球运动—竞赛规则—
2023 Ⅳ. ①G845.4

中国国家版本馆CIP数据核字(2023)第150164号

网球竞赛规则. 2023

中国网球协会　审定
出版发行：人民体育出版社
印　　装：三河市紫恒印装有限公司

开　本：850×1168　32开本　　印　张：5　　字　数：123千字
版　次：2023年12月第1版　　印　次：2025年11月第2次印刷
书　号：ISBN 978-7-5009-6350-9
印　数：10,001—13,300册
定　价：28.00元


购买本社图书，如遇有缺损页可与发行与市场营销部联系
联系电话：（010）67151482
社　　址：北京市东城区体育馆路8号（100061）
网　　址：https://books.sports.cn/

# 出版说明

此版《网球竞赛规则（2023）》是国际网球联合会2023年修订的最新版本，由中国网球协会组织有关人员进行翻译，并经中国网球协会审定在全国各级各类比赛中执行。

为了提高网球工作者的英语水平，我们在中文版规则后附上英文版全文，以供参考。

对于本书在翻译、校对过程中存在的不妥及疏漏之处，敬请读者提出宝贵的意见和建议，以便我们在今后修订时予以完善。

参与本规则译校与审定工作的有白喜林、吕亮、周文学、王玉瑾、殷剑巍、黄珊等同志。此外，人民体育出版社对本书出版、发行给予大力支持和帮助，在此一并致谢。

中国网球协会

2023年8月

# 目 录

# 前 言

国际网球联合会（简称“国际网联”）是网球竞赛的管理机构，其责任和义务是通过制定网球竞赛规则，维护网球运动的公平性。

国际网联设立网球规则委员会，通过持续监督网球竞赛及其规则来履行这项职责。该委员会在必要时向国际网联董事会提交修改意见，再由后者提交至国际网联年度代表大会，对网球规则的修改作最终认定。

附录V列举了经批准的备选程序和计分方法。此外，国际网联可以主动或在有关方提出申请时，批准在一段时间内、于部分赛事中尝试对规则进行部分改动。此类改动并未收录在已出版的规则当中，并且须在试行期结束后向国际网联提交报告。

**注：** 当《网球竞赛规则》的英语版本与其他语言译本之间存在任何不一致时，应以英语版本为准。

# 网球规则

## 1. 场地

网球场地为长方形，长度为23.77米（78英尺），单打比赛的场地宽度为8.23米（27英尺），双打比赛场地的宽度为10.97米（36英尺）。

场地由一条悬挂在绳索或金属绳上的球网从中间处分隔开，所使用的绳索或金属绳附着或悬挂在1.07米（3.5英尺）高的两根网柱上。球网应充分伸展开，填满两个网柱之间的空间，网孔的大小应确保球不能从中间穿过。球网中心的高度应为0.914米（3英尺），并且用中心带向下绷紧固定，绳索或金属绳和球网的上端应当用一条网带包裹住，中心带和网带均应完全为白色。

- 绳索或金属绳的最大直径应为0.8厘米（0.33英寸）。
- 中心带的最大宽度应为5厘米（2英寸）。
- 球网两侧的网带宽度应当在5厘米（2英寸）至6.35厘米（2.5英寸）之间。

双打比赛中，每侧网柱的中心应与双打场地外沿相距0.914米（3英尺）。

单打比赛中，如果使用单打球网，每侧网柱的中心应与单打场地外沿相距0.914米（3英尺）。如果使用双打球网，则球网要用两根高1.07米（3.5英尺）的单打支柱支撑，每侧单打支柱的中心与单打场地外沿相距0.914米（3英尺）。

- 网柱的边长/直径不应超过15厘米（6英寸）。
- 单打支柱的边长/直径不应超过7.5厘米（3英寸）。
- 网柱和单打支柱不能高出绳索2.5厘米（1英寸）以上。

球场两端的界线称为底线，两侧的界线称为边线。

在两条单打边线之间距球网6.40米（21英尺）处画两条与球网平行的线，这两条线称为发球线。球网每一边的发球线和球网之间的区域，被一条发球中线分成相同的两个部分，称为发球区。发球中线应当和单打边线平行并且与两条边线的距离相等。

每一条底线都被一条长10厘米（4英寸）的中点分为相等的两部分，中点要画在场地内并且和单打边线平行。

- 发球中线和中点的宽度为5厘米（2英寸）。
- 场上其他线的宽度均应为2.5厘米（1英寸）到5厘米（2英寸），但底线的最大宽度可以达到10厘米（4英寸）。

场地的所有测量均应以线的外沿为准，场地上所有线的颜色必须相同，并且和场地的颜色有明显的区别。

除附录Ⅳ中的规定外，球场、球网、中心带、网带、网柱或单打支柱上均不允许有广告。

除上述场地外，附录Ⅶ中提到的“红球”和“橙球”场地可以用于10岁及以下组别的比赛。

**注：**底线和后挡板之间，以及边线和侧挡板之间的最短距离标准可参见附录Ⅸ。

## 2. 永久固定物

场地上的永久固定物，不仅包括后挡板、侧挡板、观众、观众看台和座位、所有场地周围和上方的其他固定物，还包括处于各自规定位置的主裁判、司线员、司网裁判和球童。

在使用双打球网和单打支柱的场地上进行单打比赛时，网柱、单打支柱外侧的球网属于永久固定物，而不能视其为网柱或球网的一部分。

## 3. 球

网球规则批准的比赛用球必须符合附录 I 的具体要求。

国际网联负责裁决某种球或模型是否符合附录 I 的标准，以及是否可以批准用于比赛。国际网联既可以主动作出此类裁决，也可以根据相关方的申请裁决，包括运动员、器材生产厂商、国家网球协会或其会员等。此类申请与裁决应当按照国际网联相应的审查与听证程序来进行（参见附录XI）。

赛事组织方必须在赛前公布：

a. 比赛用球的数量（2个、3个、4个或6个）；

b. 换球方案（如果有的话）。

如果换球，可采用以下方式中的任何一种：

i. 规定某单数局结束后换球。在这种情况下，由于热身活动用球的原因，比赛中第一次换球必须比规定的局数提前两局进行。平局决胜局在换球时算作一局，平局决胜局开始前不应换球。在这种情况下，换球应当推迟到下一盘第二局开始前；

ii. 在一盘开始前换球。

如果球在活球期破裂，这一分应当重赛。

**判例1：** 如果在一分结束后发现球变软，这一分是否应重赛？

**答案：** 如果球只是变软而没有破裂，这一分不应重赛。

**注：** 在按照网球规则进行的比赛中，任何用球都必须是由国际网联发布的已被列入官方目录的批准用球。

## 4. 球拍

网球规则中批准的比赛用拍必须符合附录Ⅱ的具体要求。

国际网联负责裁决某种球拍或模型是否符合附录Ⅱ的标准，以及是否可以批准用于比赛。国际网联既可以主动作出此类裁决，也可以根据相关方的申请裁决，包括运动员、器材生产厂商、国家网球协会或其会员等。此类申请与裁决应当按照国际网联相应的审查与听证程序来进行（参见附录Ⅺ）。

**判例1：** 球拍击球面是否允许有一套以上的拍弦？

**答案：** 不允许，规则中提及只能有一组交叉弦（参见附录Ⅱ）。

**判例2：** 如果弦穿在一个以上的平面上，是否可以认为拍弦是大体一致和平整的？

**答案：** 不可以。

**判例3：**减振器是否可以安装在拍弦上，如果可以，应当安装在什么位置？

**答案：**可以，但只能安装在交叉弦组成的样式之外。

**判例4：**在一分未结束时，运动员的拍弦意外断裂，他可以用这把球拍继续比下一分吗？

**答案：**可以，但赛事组织方有特别规定禁止使用时除外。

**判例5：**在比赛中的任何时候，运动员可否使用一把以上的球拍？

**答案：**不可以。

**判例6：**可以在球拍内嵌入会影响击球特性的电池吗？

**答案：**不可以，比赛中禁止使用电池、太阳能电池或其他类似的动力设备。

## 5. 局分

a. 常规局

在常规局的比赛中，应首先报发球运动员的得分，计分如下：

| | | |
|---|---|---|
| 无得分 | —— | 0 |
| 第一分 | —— | 15 |
| 第二分 | —— | 30 |
| 第三分 | —— | 40 |
| 第四分 | —— | 本局比赛结束 |

若两名运动员/队都得到三分，则比分为“平分”。“平分”后如果一名运动员/队得分，则比分为“占先”。如果

“占先”的这名运动员/队又得分，他便赢得了这一局；如果“占先”后是另一名运动员/队得分，则比分仍为“平分”。运动员/队需要在“平分”后连续获得两分，才能赢得这一局。

b. 平局决胜局

在平局决胜局中，使用数字0、1、2、3等进行计分。首先赢得7分并净胜对手两分的运动员/队赢得这一局和这一盘。必要时决胜局必须持续进行，直到一方运动员/队净胜对手两分为止。

轮及发球的运动员在平局决胜局中首先发第一分球，随后的两分由他的对手发球（在双打比赛中，对方队中轮及发球的运动员进行发球）。此后，每一名运动员/队轮流连续发两分球，直到平局决胜局结束（在双打比赛中，队内发球顺序应与该盘发球顺序相同）。

在平局决胜局中应当轮及首先发球的运动员/队，在下一盘的第一局首先接发球。

其他获批的备选计分方法可参见附录V。

## 6. 盘分

盘分有不同的计分方法。主要的计分方法是“长盘制”和“平局决胜制” 两种。比赛中可以使用其中任何一种计分方法，但必须在赛前宣布。如果使用的是“平局决胜制”的计分方法，还必须声明决胜盘将采用“平局决胜制”还是“长盘制”。

a. “长盘制”

先赢得6局并净胜对手两局的运动员/队才赢得一盘。必要时一盘必须持续进行，直到一方运动员/队净胜对手两局为止。

b. “平局决胜制”

先赢得6局并净胜对手两局的运动员/队才赢得一盘。如果局分达到6：6时，则须进行“平局决胜局”。

其他获批的备选计分方法可参见附录V。

## 7. 赛制

比赛可以采用三盘两胜制，先赢得两盘的运动员/队赢得比赛；或采用五盘三胜制，先赢得三盘的运动员/队赢得比赛。

其他获批的备选计分方法可参见附录V。

## 8. 发球员和接发球员

运动员/队应当分别站于球网两侧。发球员是指发出第一分球的运动员，接发球员是指准备回击发球的运动员。

**判例1：**接发球员可以站在线外的场地上接球吗?

**答案：**可以。接发球员可以站在本侧的场地内或场地外的任何位置接球。

## 9. 站位和发球的选择

在准备活动开始前，通过掷币的方式决定比赛的第一局的站位、发球/接发球权。掷币获胜的运动员/队可以选择：

a. 在比赛的第一局中发球或接发球，在这种情况下，对手应选择第一局的场地站位；或

b. 选择比赛第一局的场地站位，在这种情况下，对手应选择发球或接发球；或

c. 要求对手做出以上任意一种选择。

**判例1：**如果准备活动被中断，运动员离开了场地，双方运动员/队是否有重新选择的权利？

**答案：**是的，原掷币结果仍然有效，但是双方运动员/队都有权利重新选择。

## 10. 交换场地

运动员应在每一盘的第一局、第三局和随后的每一个单数局结束后交换场地。运动员还应在每一盘结束后交换场地，但当一盘结束后双方所得局数之和为偶数时除外，在此情况下运动员须在下一盘第一局结束后交换场地。

在平局决胜局中，运动员应在每6分后交换场地。

其他获批的备选方案可参见附录Ⅴ。

## 11. 活球

除非呼报发球失误或重赛，从球被发球员击出的一刻开始，直到该分分出胜负为止，球处于活球状态。

## 12. 压线球

如果球压到了场地界线，那么视为这个球落在由该界线组成的场地区域之内。

## 13. 球触及永久固定物

如果活球落在正确的场地内后触到了永久固定物，则击出该球的运动员赢得该分；如果活球在落地前触到了永久固定物，则击出该球的运动员失分。

## 14. 发球次序

在常规局结束后，该局的接发球员在下一局中发球，该局的发球员在下一局中接发球。

双打比赛中，在每一盘第一局开始前，由先发球的一队决定哪一名运动员先在该局发球。同样，在第二局开始前，他们的对手也应当决定由谁在该局先发球。第一局发球员的搭档在第三局发球，第二局发球员的搭档在第四局发球。这个轮换次序一直延续到该盘结束。

## 15. 双打的接发球次序

在每一盘的第一局，首先接发球的一队要决定哪一名运动员在该局的第一分接发球。同样，在第二局开始前，他们的对手也应当决定哪一名运动员在该局的第一分接发球。第一分接发球运动员的搭档应当在本局的第二分接发球，这一次序一直延续到该局和该盘结束。接发球员接完发球后，该队中的任何一名运动员都可以回击球。

**判例1：** 双打比赛可以允许一名运动员单独和对手进行比赛吗？

**答案：** 不可以。

## 16. 发球动作

在即将做出发球动作前，发球员必须静止站在底线后（即远离球网的一侧），双脚位于中点的假定延长线和边线的假定延长线之间。

然后，发球员应当用手将球向任意方向抛出，并在球落地前用球拍将球击出。在球拍击到球或挥空的那一刻，视为整个发球动作已经完成。对于只能使用一只手臂的运动员，可以用球拍完成抛球。

## 17. 发球程序

在常规发球局中，发球员在每一局都应当从场地的右半区开始，交替在场地的两个半区发球。

在平局决胜局中，第一分球应当从场地的右半区发出，然后交替在场地的两个半区发球。

发出的球应当越过球网，在接发球员回击发球之前落到对角方向的发球区内。

## 18. 脚误

在进行发球动作期间，发球员不得：

a. 通过走动或跑动来改变位置，但允许脚步轻微移动；或

b. 任何一只脚触及底线或场地内的地面；或

c. 任何一只脚触及边线假定延长线外的地面；或

d. 任何一只脚触及中点的假定延长线。

如果发球员违反了这些规定就是一次“脚误”。

**判例1：**在单打比赛中，发球员可否站在底线后的单打边线与双打边线之间的位置发球？

**答案：**不可以。

**判例2：**发球过程中是否允许发球员的一只脚或者双脚离开地面？

**答案：**可以。

## 19. 发球失误

下列情况为发球失误：

a. 发球员违反了规则第16、17或18条；或

b. 发球员试图击球但未能击中；或

c. 发出的球在落地前碰到了永久固定物、单打支柱或网

柱；或

d. 发出的球触到了发球员或发球员的搭档，或其穿戴、携带的任何物品。

**判例1：**在发球时，发球员抛球后决定不击球而接住球，这是一次发球失误吗？

**答案：**不是。运动员抛球后决定不击球，可以手或球拍将球接住，或让球落地。

**判例2：**单打比赛在有网柱和单打支柱的场地上进行时，发出的球击中单打支柱后落在了有效的发球区内，这是一次发球失误吗？

**答案：**是。

## 20. 第二发球

如果第一发球失误，发球员应当立即从同一半区再发一次，除非第一发球是从错误的半区发出的。

## 21. 何时发球和接发球

发球员应在接发球员做好准备后再发球。但是，接发球员应当按照发球员合理的发球节奏来比赛，并在发球员准备发球时，在合理的时间内做好接发球的准备。

接发球员如果试图回击发球，则被认为已做好准备。如果证实接发球员确未做好准备，那么该次发球也不能被判为失误。

## 22. 重发球

如果出现下列情况，应当重发球：

a. 发出的球触到了球网、中心带或网带后落在有效发球区内；或在球触到了球网、中心带或网带后，在落地前触到了接发球员或其搭档，或他们穿戴的、携带的任何物品；或

b. 当球发出时，接发球员未做好准备。

在重发球时，发球员只需重发该次发球，但是不能取消重发球之前的发球失误。

获批的其他备选程序可参见附录Ⅴ。

## 23. 重赛

除对第二发球呼报重赛是指重发该次发球外，在所有其他情况下，当呼报重赛时，这一分必须重赛。

**判例1：** 在活球期间，另一个球滚入场地内。裁判员呼报重赛。发球员之前有一次发球失误，此时发球员应获得第一发球还是第二发球的权利？

**答案：** 第一发球，这完整的一分必须重赛。

## 24. 运动员失分

如果出现下列情况，运动员将失分：

a. 发球员连续两次发球失误；或

b. 在活球状态下，运动员在球连续两次触地前未能将球回击过网；或

c. 在活球状态下，运动员回击的球落到有效击球区外的地面或落地前触碰到有效击球区外的其他物体；或

d. 在活球状态下，运动员回击的球在落地前触到永久固定物；或

e. 接发球员在发球员发出的球尚未落地时回击；或

f. 运动员故意用他的球拍托带或接住处于活球状态的球，或故意用球拍触球超过一次；或

g. 在活球状态下的任何时候，运动员或他的球拍（无论球拍是否在他手中），或他穿戴的、携带的任何物品触到球网、网柱/单打支柱、绳索或金属绳、中心带或网带，或他对手的场地；或

h. 运动员在球尚未过网时击球；或

i. 在活球状态下，除运动员手中的球拍外，球触及运动员的身体或他穿戴的、携带的任何物品；　或

j. 在活球状态下，球触到了运动员的球拍，但球拍不在他的手中；或

k. 在活球状态下，运动员故意并实质性地改变了球拍的形状；或

l. 双打比赛中，在一次回击球时，同队的两名运动员都触到了球。

**判例1：**发球员在第一次发球后，球拍从他的手中脱落，在球落地前球拍碰到了球网。这是一次发球失误，还是发球员失分？

**答案：**发球员失分，因为在活球期间球拍触及球网。

**判例2：**发球员在第一次发球后，球拍从他的手中脱落，在球触及有效发球区以外的地面后球拍碰到球网。这是一次发球失误，还是发球员失分？

**答案：**这是一次发球失误，因为球拍触及球网时，球已经不处于活球状态了。

**判例3：**双打比赛中，接发球运动员的搭档在对方发出的球触及有效发球区以外的地面前触及球网，应当如何判定？

**答案：**接发球方失分，因为活球期间接发球运动员的搭档触及球网。

**判例4：**运动员在击球前或击球后越过球网的假定延长线，运动员是否失分？

**答案：**在这两种情况下，如果运动员没有触及对方的场地，都不失分。

**判例5：**活球期间运动员可否越过球网进入对方的场地？

**答案：**不可以，这名运动员失分。

**判例6：**活球期间运动员抛拍击球，球和球拍均落入对方的场地，对方未能击到球，哪一名运动员赢得该分？

**答案：**抛拍击球的运动员失分。

**判例7：**球被发出后，在触地前刚好击中接发球员，或双打接发球员的搭档，哪一名运动员赢得该分？

**答案：**发球运动员赢得该分，除非裁判呼报了重发球。

**判例8：**运动员站在场地外回击或接住还未落地的球，并且宣称赢得该分，因为球明显会飞出有效场地。

**答案：**运动员失分。除非运动员做出了有效的回球，此时应继续比赛。

## 25. 有效回击

下列情况属于有效回击：

a. 球触到了球网、网柱/单打支柱、绳索或金属绳、中心带或网带并且越过球网后落到有效场地内；规则第2条和第24条（d款）除外；或

b. 在活球状态下，球落在有效场地内后旋转或被风吹回过网，运动员越过球网击球，将球击打到有效场地内，并且没有违反规则第24条的规定；或

c. 球从网柱外侧绕过并落在有效场地内，无论该球是否高于球网，即使触到网柱，规则第2条和第24条（d款）除外；或

d. 球从单打支柱及其相邻网柱之间的绳索下面穿过而又没有触及球网、绳索或网柱，并且落在有效场地内；或

e. 运动员在回击自己球网一侧的球后，球拍随球过网，球落入有效场地内；或

f. 在活球状态下，运动员击出的球碰到了有效场地内的另一个球。

**判例1：**运动员回击的球击中单打支柱并落入有效场地内，这是否为有效击球？

**答案：**是有效击球。但如果这是一次发球，则为一次发球失误。

**判例2：**在活球状态下，球击中有效场地内的另一个球，应当如何判定？

**答案：** 继续比赛。然而，如果裁判员此时不能确定回击的球是否为本回合使用的球，则这一分应当重赛。

## 26. 干扰

如果运动员在某一分的比赛中受到对手的故意干扰，那么这名受干扰的运动员赢得此分。

然而，如果运动员在某一分的比赛中受到对手非故意的或者自身无法控制的因素干扰时（场地上的永久固定物除外），这一分应当重赛。

**判例1：** 无意的连击是否为干扰？

**答案：** 不是，参见规则第24条（f款）。

**判例2：** 一名运动员认为他的对手受到干扰进而停止比赛，这是否为一次干扰？

**答案：** 不是，这名运动员失分。

**判例3：** 比赛中球击中飞过球场上空的鸟，这是否为一次干扰？

**答案：** 是的，这一分应当重赛。

**判例4：** 一分开始前已经在运动员这一侧场地内的一个球或其他物体，在这一分中干扰了该名运动员，这是否为一次干扰？

**答案：** 不是。

**判例5：** 在双打比赛中，发球员或接发球员的搭档站在何处？

**答案：** 发球员或接发球员的搭档可以站在球网一侧己方

场地内或场地外的任何位置。然而，如果运动员干扰了对方，那么将使用干扰规则。

## 27. 更正错误

原则上，当比赛中发现违反网球规则的错误时，已经完成的所有比分都有效，发现的错误应当按照如下条款更正：

a. 在常规局或平局决胜局中，如果运动员从错误的半区发球，此错误一经发现应当立即更正，发球员要按照场上的比分从正确的半区发球。发现错误前的发球失误仍有效。

b. 在常规局或平局决胜局中，如果双方运动员出现了左右侧场地站位错误，则此错误一经发现应当立即更正，发球员要按照场上的比分从正确的一边场地发球。

c. 在常规局中如果运动员的发球次序错误，此错误一经发现应立即更正，由本应发球的运动员发球。然而，如果发现错误前该局已经结束，则发球的次序按照已改变的次序进行。在这种情况下，此后的所有换球必须比原规定的局数推后一局进行。

发现发球次序错误前，对手有一次发球失误，该发球失误不予计算。

在双打比赛中，如果同队的两名运动员出现发球次序错误，则发现错误前的发球失误仍有效。

d. 在平局决胜局中，运动员发球次序错误，如果在双数比分结束后发现该错误，则应当立即纠正。如果在单数比分结束后发现该错误，那么发球次序就按照已改变的次序进行。

发现发球次序错误前，对手有一次发球失误，该发球失误不予计算。

在双打比赛中，如果同队的两名运动员出现发球次序错误，则发现错误前的发球失误仍有效。

e. 在双打比赛的常规局或平局决胜局中，如果接发球次序错误，则按照已发生的错误次序继续进行，直到这一局结束。在这一盘的下一次接发球局，运动员应当恢复原始的接发球次序。

f. 赛前规定为“长盘制”的比赛，但是在局数6：6时错误地开始了一个“平局决胜局”，如果该局仅进行了一分，则此错误应立即更正；如果发现错误时第二分的比赛已经开始，则这盘比赛将按照“平局决胜制”继续进行。

g. 赛前规定为“平局决胜制”的比赛，但是在局数6：6时错误地开始了常规局的比赛，如果此时仅进行了第一分，则此错误应立即更正；如果发现错误时第二分的比赛已经开始，则这盘比赛将按照“长盘制”继续进行，直到双方的局数达到8：8时（或更高分值的偶数平局时）再进行“平局决胜局”。

h. 赛前规定决胜盘采用“平盘决胜局制”，但是在决胜盘错误地开始了“平局决胜制”或“长盘制”的比赛，如果此时仅进行了第一分，则此错误应立即更正；如果发现错误时第二分的比赛已经开始，则这一盘比赛继续进行，直到一名运动员/队赢得3局（赢得这一盘），或者局分2：2时，再进行“平盘决胜局”。然而，如果在第五局的第二分比赛开始后才发现错误，则这一盘将以“平局决胜制”继续比赛（参考附录V）。

i. 如果没有按照正确的顺序换球，那么要等到应该使用新球发球的运动员/队的下一个发球轮次前更换新球。此后的换球顺序仍然按照最初的规定，在达到既定的换球局数后进行更换。在一局比赛进行过程中不能换球。

## 28. 场上技术官员的作用

对于指派了技术官员的比赛，技术官员的作用和职责参见附录Ⅵ。

## 29. 连续比赛

原则上，比赛从第一个球发出开始直到结束应当连续地进行。

a. 分与分之间，最长间隔时间为25秒。运动员在一局结束后交换场地时，最长间隔时间为90秒。但是，在每盘的第一局结束后和在平局决胜局中运动员换场地时，比赛应连续进行，没有休息。

在每一盘结束后，盘间最长间隔时间为120秒。

最长间隔时间是指从一分球结束时开始，直到下一分第一发球击出时为止。

赛事组织方可以向国际网联申请延长单数局结束时运动员交换场地的90秒间隔时间，以及盘间的120秒间隔时间。

b. 如果运动员的服装、鞋子或必要的装备（不包括球拍）等，因不可控制的原因损坏或需要更换，可以给予运动员合理的额外时间去解决这些问题。

c. 不能给予一名运动员额外的时间恢复体力。但是，当运动员出现可以治疗的伤病时，可以获得一次3分钟的医疗暂停来治疗伤病。如果赛前宣布相关规定，运动员还可以获得一定次数的去洗手间/更换衣服的时间。

d. 如果赛事组织方在赛前宣布相关规定，整场比赛允许有一次最长为10分钟的休息时间，可以在五盘三胜制的第三盘结束之后，或在三盘两胜制的第二盘结束之后采用。

e. 除非赛事组织方事先另有规定，否则准备活动时间最长不超过5分钟。

## 30. 指导

对运动员进行任何方式（包括但不限于可听见、可看见）的交流、建议或各种指示都被认为是指导。

在团体赛中，如果领队或教练员坐在场内，运动员可以在每盘结束后或单数局结束交换场地的休息时间内接受指导，但是在每一盘的第一局结束后和平局决胜局交换场地时不能接受指导。

在其他的任何比赛中，运动员都不能接受指导。

**判例1：**如果指导是不易察觉的信号，运动员可以接受这样的指导吗？

**答案：**不可以。

**判例2：**比赛暂停期间，运动员可以接受指导吗？

**答案：**可以。

**判例3：** 在比赛期间，是否允许运动员接受场上指导？

**答案：** 执行机构可以向国际网联申请允许场上指导。在允许场上指导的赛事中，指定的教练员可以进入场地，按照执行机构制定的程序对运动员进行指导。

## 31. 运动员分析技术

网球规则批准的运动员分析技术必须符合附录Ⅲ的具体要求。

此类设备是否被批准使用，由国际网联负责裁决。国际网联既可以主动作出此类裁决，也可以根据相关方（包括运动员、器材生产厂商、国家网球协会及其会员等）的申请进行裁决。此类申请与裁决应当按照国际网联相应的审查与听证程序进行（参见附录Ⅺ）。

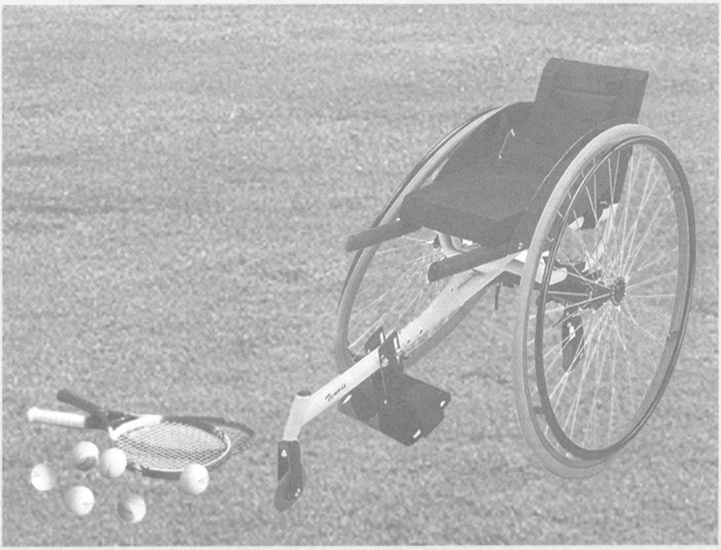

# 轮椅网球规则

除以下特殊规定外，轮椅网球运动遵照国际网联制定的网球规则执行。

a. 两跳规则

轮椅网球允许运动员在球落地两次后击球，运动员必须在球第三次落地前回击，球第二次落地可以落在场地内或场地外。

b. 轮椅

轮椅被认为是身体的一部分，所有涉及有关运动员身体的规则对于轮椅同样适用。

c. 发球

发球应当按照以下方式进行：

i. 在开始发球前，发球运动员必须处静止状态。在击球前发球员可允许向前推一下轮椅。

ii. 在整个发球过程中，发球员轮椅的轮子须在底线后面、边线和中心标志假定延长线之间的区域。

iii. 如果四肢瘫痪的运动员不能用常规动作完成抛球，则可以由自己或他人抛球，并可以在球落地后击球。在这种情况下，整场比赛中必须使用同样的抛球方法。

d. 运动员失分

如果出现下列情况，则运动员失分：

i. 未能在球第三次落地前将球回击过网；或

ii. 除第f条的情形外，活球期间，运动员在发球、击球、转向或停轮椅时，用脚或下肢触地或碰到轮子；或

iii. 在击球时没有保持臀部一侧与轮椅接触。

e. 轮椅

在依据轮椅网球规则进行的比赛中，所使用的轮椅应当符合以下具体要求：

i. 轮椅可以使用任何材质，但不能反光，不能给对手造成干扰。

ii. 轮椅只能有一个驱动轮。不可以为轮椅增加动力装置，如操纵杆或传动装置。在正常比赛中，车轮不能对场地表面造成永久性痕迹或破坏。

iii. 除第e条（v 款）规定外，运动员只能使用轮子（包括驱动轮）推动轮椅。不能使用方向盘、制动、传动装置或其他设备辅助操作轮椅，包括能量储备系统。

iv. 座椅的高度（包括坐垫）应该固定，在活球期间，运动员的臀部应当与座椅保持接触。可以使用绑带将运动员固定在轮椅上。

v. 符合国际网联分级规则第10条规定的运动员可以使用电动轮椅。电动轮椅向任意方向的移动速度不能超过每小时15公里，并且只能由运动员本人操作。

vi. 因合理的医疗原因，可于拟参加国际网联批准的比赛前至少60天，向国际网联体育科学与医学委员会申请对轮椅进行改动。如未获批准，可以依据国际网联轮椅网球规程第三章进行申诉。

f. 用脚推动轮椅

i. 由于身体的原因，运动员不能通过车轮驱动轮椅，那么他可以使用一只脚驱动轮椅。

ii. 尽管上述第f条（i 款）允许运动员使用一只脚驱动轮椅，但以下情况中运动员的脚不能接触地面：

a）在向前挥拍期间，包括球拍击球时；

b）从做发球动作开始直到击球时。

iii.运动员违反了这条规则就失分。

g. 轮椅网球/健全人的比赛

当轮椅运动员和健全人进行单打或双打比赛时，轮椅运动员要遵守轮椅网球规则，而健全人则要遵守健全人网球规则。在这种情况下，轮椅运动员击球前允许球落地两次，而健全人击球前只允许球落地一次。

**注：**下肢包括臀部、髋部、大腿、小腿、踝和足。

# 网球规则的修改原则

网球规则的官方正式文本始终使用英文表述，只有在国际网联的年度代表大会上可以变更或解释本规则。修改决议须根据国际网联章程第17条（决议通知）的规定提交至国际网联，该决议或类似性质的内容须通过投票表决，得票率超过2/3方可生效。

规则的任何变更都要从下一年的1月1日起生效，大会通过表决另行规定的除外。

董事会有权在下一年的年度代表大会批准之前，对所有的紧急问题作出解释。

未经年度代表大会一致同意，任何时候都不得对本规则进行修改。

# 附 录

## 附录Ⅰ 球

附录Ⅰ中的所有测量值，均优先采用国际标准单位。

a. 除3阶（红色）海绵球外，网球的表面应为同种纺织物，接缝处不应有缝线。

b. 球的规定应当符合下表，或第d条的要求。

| | 1型球（快速） | 2型球（中速）[1] | 3型球（慢速）[2] | 高海拔型球[3] |
|---|---|---|---|---|
| 重量（质量） | 56.0~59.4克（1.975~2.095盎司） | 56.0~59.4克（1.975~2.095盎司） | 56.0~59.4克（1.975~2.095盎司） | 56.0~59.4克（1.975~2.095盎司） |
| 尺寸 | 6.54~6.86厘米（2.57~2.70英寸） | 6.54~6.86厘米（2.57~2.70英寸） | 7.00~7.30厘米（2.76~2.87英寸） | 6.54~6.86厘米（2.57~2.70英寸） |
| 弹性 | 138~151厘米（54~60英寸） | 135~147厘米（53~58英寸） | 135~147厘米（53~58英寸） | 122~135厘米（48~53英寸） |
| 压缩形变[4] | 0.56~0.74厘米（0.220~0.291英寸） | 0.56~0.74厘米（0.220~0.291英寸） | 0.56~0.74厘米（0.220~0.291英寸） | 0.56~0.74厘米（0.220~0.291英寸） |
| 反弹形变[4] | 0.74~1.08厘米（0.291~0.425英寸） | 0.80~1.08厘米（0.315~0.425英寸） | 0.80~1.08厘米（0.315~0.425英寸） | 0.80~1.08厘米（0.315~0.425英寸） |
| 颜色 | 白色或黄色 | 白色或黄色 | 白色或黄色 | 白色或黄色 |

**注：**

1. 中速球可以是加压的，也可以是低压的。低压球的压强不得大于7千帕（1 PSI），可以用于海拔1219米（4000英尺）的地方，并应在与比赛地海拔高度相同的地方放置60天以上。

2. 慢速球也推荐用于海拔高度为1219米（4000英尺）以上的各种类型场地的比赛。

3. 高海拔型球为加压球，是专门用于海拔1219米（4000英尺）以上高度的比赛用球。

4. 形变的数据是球的3个轴方向读数的平均值，任何两次数据之间的差不能大于0.08厘米（0.031英寸）。

c. 此外，规则b中的所有类型的球都要符合下表中关于耐久性的要求：

| | 重量（质量） | 弹性 | 压缩形变 | 反弹形变 |
|---|---|---|---|---|
| 最大变化幅度[1] | 0.4克<br>（0.014盎司） | 4.0厘米<br>（1.6英寸） | 0.08厘米<br>（0.031英寸） | 0.10厘米<br>（0.039英寸） |

**注：**

以上各项属性在耐久性测试下的最大变化幅度参见现有版本的《国际网联批准用球、场地分类和获准场地》。耐久性测试使用实验室设备模拟九局比赛的效果。

d. 只有以下表格中列举的球可用于10岁及以下年龄组的网球比赛：

| | 三阶（红色）<br>海绵 | 三阶（红色）<br>标准 | 二阶（橙色）<br>标准 | 一阶（绿色）<br>标准 |
|---|---|---|---|---|
| 质量（重量） | 25.0~43.0克（0.882~1.517盎司） | 36.0~49.0克（1.270~1.728盎司） | 36.0~46.9克（1.270~1.654盎司） | 47.0~51.5克（1.658~1.817盎司） |
| 尺寸 | 8.00~9.00厘米（3.15~3.54英寸） | 7.00~8.00厘米（2.76~3.15英寸） | 6.00~6.86厘米（2.36~2.70英寸） | 6.30~6.86厘米（2.48~2.70英寸） |
| 弹性 | 85~105厘米（33~41英寸） | 90~105厘米（35~41英寸） | 105~120厘米（41~47英寸） | 120~135厘米（47~53英寸） |
| 压缩形变[1] | — | — | 1.40~1.65厘米（0.551~0.650英寸） | 0.80~1.05厘米（0.315~0.413英寸） |
| 颜色[2] | 不限 | 红加黄，或黄色带红点 | 橙加黄，或黄色带橙色点 | 黄色带绿点 |

**注：**

1. 形变的数据是球的3个轴方向读数的平均值，任何两次数据差无要求。对反弹形变无具体要求。

2. 球上点的尺寸和位置应合理。

e. 所有针对弹性、质量、尺寸、形变和耐久性的测试应当按照现有版本《国际网联批准用球、场地类型和获准场地》的相关规定进行。

# 球场速度分级

国际网联用于确认球场面层速度的检测方法是国际网联CS01/02试验法（国际网联球场速度分级），在国际网联出版的《国际网联网球场面层测试方法指南》中有具体说明。

球场面层按照国际网联球场地面速度分级从0到29为第1类（慢速）。符合此类分级的场地类型包括大部分红土球场和其他疏松石土的球场。

球场面层按照国际网联球场地面速度分级从30到34为第2类（中等偏慢）；速度分级从35到39为第3类（中速）。符合此类分级的场地类型包括大多数丙烯酸铺覆的硬地球场和部分地毯球场。

球场面层按照国际网联球场地面速度分级从40到44为第4类（中等偏快）；速度分级45及以上的为第5类（快速）。符合此类分级的场地类型包括天然草地球场、人造草地球场和部分地毯球场。

**判例1：**在不同的场地上应当分别使用哪种类型的球？

**答案：**可以使用3种符合网球规则的球。但是：

a. 1型球（快速）用于慢速场地。

b. 2型球（中速）用于中等偏慢、中等或中等偏快的场地。

c. 3型球（慢速）用于快速场地。

**注：**除第b条列举的球以外，一阶（绿色）球可用于所有级别的比赛中，但以下比赛除外：获得世界排名的职业网球赛事，戴维斯杯和比利·简·金杯，奥运会和残奥会网球比赛，由

国际网联和所属地区网协批准的世界男子、女子、青少年网球巡回赛和团体赛，国际网联元老巡回赛和团体赛，以及国际网联轮椅网球巡回赛和团体赛。

每个国家网协都有权决定哪项全国网球比赛将使用一阶（绿色）球。

# 附录Ⅱ　球　拍

附录Ⅱ中的所有测量值，均优先采用国际标准单位。

a. 球拍由拍框和拍弦组成。拍框包括拍柄、拍头（和拍颈）。拍头即球拍中与拍弦连接的部分。拍柄即与拍头相连，运动员正常手持球拍的部分。拍颈指连接拍头与拍柄的部分。

b. 球拍的击球面是指交叉弦的主要部分，击球面应当平整，由连接在拍框上的弦组成，拍弦在交叉的地方应当是相互交织或相互结合的；交叉弦应当大体一致，尤其是中心的密度不能低于其他部分的密度。球拍的设计和穿弦方式应使球拍两面的击球特性完全一致。

c. 球拍的总长度不能超过73.7厘米（29.0英寸），总宽度不能超过31.7厘米（12.5英寸）。以拍柄中轴线为基准测量时，击球面的总长度不能超过39.4厘米（15.5英寸），以拍柄中轴线垂直线为基准测量时，击球面的总宽度不能超过29.2厘米（11.5英寸）。

d. 球拍上不能有任何可以从实质上改变球拍形状，或改变球拍轴方向的惯性矩，或者改变球拍物理性质从而影响球拍击球性能的物件、凸起或装置。获得批准的运动员分析技术，或用来减少或防止损耗或振动，或分配拍框重量的装置除外，但尺寸和位置必须合理并与其用途相符。

任何形式的能够改变或影响球拍性能的能源装置，都不能装进或附着在球拍上。

# 附录Ⅲ　运动员分析技术

运动员分析技术是指可以通过以下功能处理运动员表现数据的设备：

a. 录制。

b. 存储。

c. 传送。

d. 分析。

e. 以任何种类、通过任何形式与运动员沟通

运动员分析技术可以在比赛期间录制/存储信息。根据规则第30条，只有运动员可以获得此类信息。

# 附录Ⅳ　广　告

1. 在球网上，距网柱中心0.914米（3英尺）以内的区域可以放置广告，但广告不应影响运动员的视野和比赛环境。

执行机构可以在球网下部，距离球网顶端至少0.51米（20英寸）的位置放置一个非商业标识，但不能影响运动员的视野和比赛环境。

2. 在场地后侧和两侧可以放置广告及其他标志或物体，但不能影响运动员的视野或比赛环境。

3. 在场地界线之外的地面上可以设置广告及其他标志或物体，但不能影响运动员的视野或比赛环境。

4. 虽然有上述第1、2、3条的规定，但设置在球网上、场地后侧和两侧、场地界线之外地面上的广告，颜色不能是白色、黄色或其他亮色，以免影响运动员的视野或比赛环境。

5. 在球场界线以内的场地表面不能有广告及其他标志或物体。

# 附录Ⅴ　备选程序和计分方法

该附录列举的备选程序和计分方法可以在比赛中使用。

## 局分（规则第5条）：

"无占先"计分法

在"无占先"的常规局的比赛中按如下方式计分，发球运动员的比分在前：

无得分　——　0

第一分　——　15

第二分　——　30

第三分　——　40

第四分　——　局比赛结束

如果双方运动员/队都赢得3分，这时的比分叫"平分"，然后进行决胜分。接发球员将选择从场地右半区还是从左半区接发球。在双打比赛中，接发球方的两名队员在决胜分时不能改变接球站位。赢得决胜分的运动员/队赢得这一局。

在混双比赛中，与发球员同性别的接发球员应当接决胜分的发球。接发球方的两名队员在决胜分时不能改变接球站位。

## 盘分（规则第6条和第7条）：

### 1. 短盘制

先赢得四局并净胜对手两局的运动员/队赢得这一盘。如果局分达到4：4，则进行“平局决胜局”的比赛。或者，如果赛事批准方同意，也可以在局分3：3时进行“平局决胜局”的比赛。

### 2. 短盘制平局决胜局

短盘制平局决胜局只能用于短盘制比赛。先赢得5分的运动员/队赢得这一局和这一盘，当比分达到4：4时，将进行决胜分。发球的次序和数量由赛事批准方决定。运动员/队只需要在第4分结束后换场地。

### 3. 平盘决胜局（七分制）

当比赛的盘分达到1：1，或在五盘三胜制的比赛中盘分达到 2：2时，则用“平盘决胜局制”代替决胜盘来决定比赛的胜负。

先赢得7分并净胜对手两分的运动员/队，将赢得“平盘决胜局”和整场比赛。

### 4. 平盘决胜局（十分制）

当比赛的盘分达到1：1，或在五盘三胜制的比赛中盘分达到2：2时，则用“平盘决胜局制”代替决胜盘来决定比赛的胜负。

先赢得10分并净胜对手两分的运动员/队，将赢得“平盘决胜局”和整场比赛。

**注：**当采用“平盘决胜局”代替决胜盘时：

- 发球顺序保持不变（规则第5条和第14条）。
- 在双打比赛中，就像每盘开始时那样，各队的发球和接发球顺序可以改变（规则第14条和第15条）。
- 在“平盘决胜局”比赛开始前，应有120秒的盘间休息。
- 即使在“平盘决胜局”前本应换新球，此时也不能换球。

## 交换场地（规则第10条）：

在“平局决胜局”中，运动员在第一分后和随后的每4分后交换场地。

## 发球中的重发（规则第22条）：

“不重发”规则

“不重发”规则与规则第22条a款中有关重发球的内容不同，这一备选的发球规则是指，被发出的球触及球网、中心带或网带后，仍为活球。经赛事批准方同意，在采用短盘制、无占先、“不重发”规则的双打比赛中，被发出的球触及球网、中心带或网带，然后落入正确的发球区时，接发球方的两名运动员均可以回击此次发球。

# 附录Ⅵ　场上技术官员的作用

裁判长对于所有涉及网球规则的问题有最终裁决权，裁判长的决定是最终裁定。

在设有主裁判的比赛中，主裁判对于在整场比赛中所有事实问题有最终裁决权。

当运动员对主裁判关于网球规则问题作出的裁决有疑问时，有权申请裁判长到场。

在设有司线员和司网裁判的比赛中，他们对自己所负责的线或球网做出全部呼报（包括脚误的呼报）。如果主裁判确定司线员或司网裁判作出非常明显的误判，主裁判有权改判。在没有司线员和司网裁判的比赛中，主裁判负责所有线和球网的呼报（包括脚误的呼报）。

如果司线员没能对场上的情况做出呼报，他应当立即向主裁判示意，主裁判应当立即对场上的情况作出裁决。如果司线员没能对场上的情况做出呼报，或比赛中没有司线员而主裁判也不能对场上的事实问题作出判决时，这一分应当重赛。

在团体比赛中，当裁判长坐在场上时，裁判长可以对任何事实问题作出最终裁决。

在主裁判认为必要或适当的任何时候，可以随时中断或暂停比赛。

在光线暗、天气或场地条件不利的情况下，裁判长也可以中断或暂停比赛。当因光线暗而暂停比赛时，应当在该盘结束，或在这一盘中的双数局结束后暂停。在比赛暂停后重新开始时，双方的比分和在场地上的位置保持不变。

裁判长和主裁判可以根据已批准实施的行为规范的要求，对于连续比赛和指导的问题作出裁决。

**判例1：**主裁判改判后给了发球员第一发球，而接发球运动员争辩说发球运动员此前有过一次发球失误，应是第二发球，此时是否应该要求裁判长到场作出裁决？

**答案：**可以。对于涉及的网球规则方面的问题（有关特定事实认定的问题），首先由场上的主裁判作出裁决。然而，当运动员不同意主裁判的裁决时，应由裁判长作出最终裁决。

**判例2：**球被呼报“出界”，但运动员声称是有效球，此时可否要求裁判长到场作出裁决？

**答案：**不可以。对于比赛中的“事实问题”（涉及的是在某一个具体事件中实际发生的事情），主裁判的决定就是最终裁决。

**判例3：**主裁判可否在比赛中一分结束后改判司线员的裁决，因为他认为在刚结束的回合中司线员作出了一个明显的误判？

**答案：**不可以。主裁判只能在司线员出现明显误判后立即改判。

**判例4：**在司线员呼报“出界”之后，一名运动员申辩他的回球是有效球。主裁判此时是否可以改判？

**答案：**不可以。主裁判绝对不能因为运动员的抗议或申诉而作出任何改判。

**判例5：**司线员呼报球“出界”，主裁判虽然认为球落在界内，但是他未能看得非常清楚。那么他是否可以更改司线员的呼报？

**答案：**不可以。主裁判只有在确信司线员作出了明显的误判时才能改判。

**判例6：**司线员是否可以在主裁判报分之后更改自己的呼报？

**答案：**可以。如果司线员认为自己犯错了，只要不是出于运动员抗议或申诉的原因，就应当尽快更正。

**判例7：**在主裁判或司线员呼报“出界”之后更正回球是有效球。正确的判罚是怎样的？

**答案：**主裁判必须决定之前的出界呼报是否干扰了双方运动员。如果是干扰，这一分应重赛。如果不是干扰，击球的运动员赢得这一分。

**判例8：**当球被风吹回过网时，运动员按照规则准备过网击打该球。他的对手妨碍了该运动员的回球动作，正确的判罚是怎样的？

**答案：**主裁判必须作出判断，如果对手有意干扰，该分应判给受到干扰的运动员，如果是无意的干扰则该分要重赛。

## 检查球印的程序

1. 检查球印只适用于红土场地。

2. 只有在一分球的最后一击，或者运动员在比赛中主动停止击球（回击后立即停止），主裁从裁判椅的角度对球的落点不能作出判定时，才能在运动员的要求下检查球印。

3. 当主裁判决定检查球印时，应当从主裁椅走下亲自检查。若不知道球印的位置，可以要求司线员帮助确定，但必须由主裁判亲自检查。

4. 当司线员和主裁判都不能确定球印的位置或球印已不清晰时，则应维持之前的呼报或改判后的结果。

5. 主裁判确定球印位置后作出的裁决为最终裁决，且不能申诉。

6. 在红土场地进行比赛时，除非主裁判十分确定，否则不应过快呼报比分。如有疑问，应当先决定是否需要检查球印然后再报分。

7. 在双打比赛中，运动员必须在主动停止击球或主裁判呼报停止击球时才能提出申诉。如果运动员向主裁判提出申诉，主裁判首先必须确定是否符合正确的申诉程序。如果不符合申诉程序或申诉时间已晚，那么主裁判可以判定对方运动队受到故意干扰。

8. 如果在主裁判作出最终裁决之前运动员擦掉了球印，那就意味着他已认可该分的呼报。

9. 运动员不可以越过球网去检查球印，否则将按照行为准则中的“违反体育道德”予以处罚。

## 电子回放的程序

在使用电子回放系统的网球赛事中，在设有该系统的场地上的比赛应当遵循以下程序。

1. 只有在一分球的最后一击，或者运动员在比赛中主动停止（回击后立即停止）时，才能允许运动员对此次判罚或改判申请查看电子回放。

2. 当对判罚或改判有疑问时，主裁判应当决定使用电子回放。然而，如果主裁判确信运动员提出的申请不合理或不及时，他可以拒绝使用电子回放。

3. 在双打比赛中，运动员必须主动停止击球，或在主裁判终止一分时提出申请。如果运动员向主裁判提出申请，主裁判必须首先确定申请是否符合正确程序。如果申请不符合程序或申请不及时，那么主裁判可以判定对方运动员队受到故意干扰，在这种情况下申请方将失分。

4. 如果电子回放系统出于某种原因不能对呼报或改判作出判定，之前的呼报或改判将保持不变。

5. 电子回放的结果是主裁判的最终裁决，且不可申诉。如果一个特定的球需要用手动的方式来查看回放，那么应由裁判长任命的回放技术官员确定需要被查看的落点。

6. 每名运动员（队）每盘允许有三（3）次挑战失败的机会，平局决胜局中增加一（1）次。在长盘决胜制的比赛中，运动员（队）在盘分6：6时以及之后的每12局将重新获得最多三（3）次挑战失败的机会。当比赛采用平盘决胜局时，这个平盘决胜局将被视为一盘，每个运动员（队）将拥有三（3）次挑战失败的机会。运动员（队）挑战成功的次数不受限制。

# 附录Ⅶ 10岁及以下年龄组的网球比赛

## 场地

除规则第1条中列出的（全尺寸）场地外，以下尺寸的场地可用于10岁及以下年龄组的网球比赛：

- 适用于10岁及以下年龄组网球比赛的“红球”场地应当为长方形，长度为10.97米（36英尺）至12.80米（42英尺），宽度为4.27米（14英尺）至6.10米（20英尺）。球网中间的高度应为0.800米（31.5英寸）至0.838米（33.0英寸）。
- “橙球”场地应为长方形，长度为17.68米（58英尺）至18.29米（60英尺），宽度为6.10米（20英尺）至8.23米（27英尺）。球网中间的高度为0.800米（31.5英寸）至0.914米（36.0英寸）。

## 球

附录Ⅰ中只有以下种类的球可以用于10岁及以下年龄组的网球比赛：

- 在红球场地上的比赛建议使用3阶（红色）球，适合年龄不超过8岁的运动员，配合使用长度不超过58.4厘米（23英寸）的球拍。
- 在橙球场地上的比赛建议使用2阶（橙色）球，适合8岁到10岁的运动员，配合使用长度为58.4厘米（23英寸）至63.5

厘米（25 英寸）的球拍。

- 在全尺寸场地上的比赛建议使用1阶（绿色）球，适合9岁至10岁的高水平运动员，配合使用长度为63.5厘米（25 英寸）至66.0厘米（26英寸）的球拍。

**注：**附录I中列出的其他类型的球不能用于10岁及以下年龄组的网球比赛。

## 计分方法

10岁及以下年龄组运动员在采用3阶（红色）、2阶（橙色）和1阶（绿色）球比赛时，可以采用网球规则（包括附录V）中规定的计分方法，也可以使用一些简短的计分方法，包括平盘决胜局一局决胜制、平盘决胜局三局两胜制/平盘决胜局、短盘一盘决胜制和常规盘一盘决胜制等。

## 计时赛

针对10岁及以下年龄组的网球比赛，赛事委员会可以设置计时赛。

# 附录Ⅷ　网球场地平面图

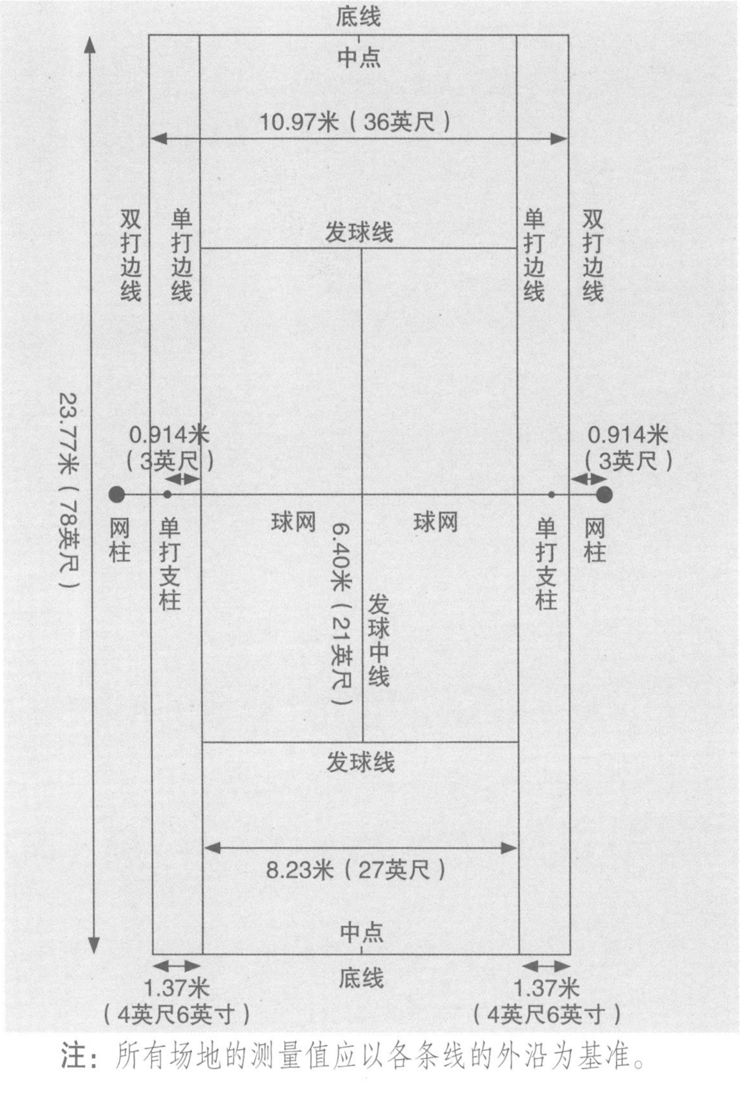


注：所有场地的测量值应以各条线的外沿为基准。

# 附录Ⅸ　关于场地绘制的建议

## 包括混合线

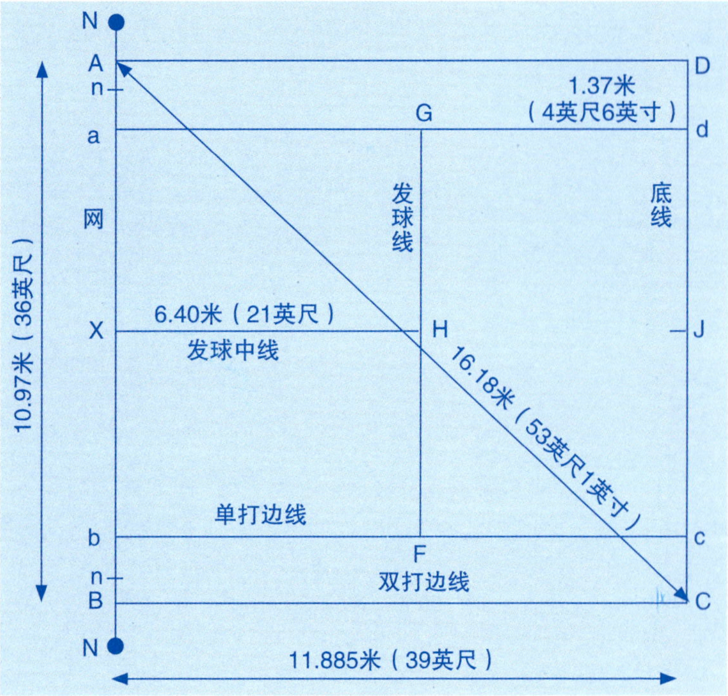


**注：**所有场地的测量值应以各条线的外沿为基准。

一般单打和双打兼用的场地画线步骤如下（单打专用场地画线步骤见注释）：

首先选择球网位置，画一长12.80米（42英尺）的直线。中点处做标记（如图所示的X点），然后由此点向两侧丈量，定点如下：

距X点各4.11米（13英尺6英寸）处为a、b点，球网于此处与单打边线相交。

距X点各5.03米（16英尺6英寸）处为n、n点，为单打支柱的位置。

距X点各5.48米（18英尺）处为A、B点，球网于此处与双打边线相交。

距X点各6.40米（21英尺）处为N、N点，为网柱的位置，即12.8米（42英尺）基准线的两端。

在A、B点加钉，并分别与两根量尺的一端相连。一根从A点向半场对角线方向量16.18米（53英尺1英寸），而另外一根从边线量为11.89米（39英尺）。将两尺相交于C点，即构成半场的一角。反向可丈量出另一角D 点。作为上述测量的检查，量好检验CD线,即底线的长度，应为10.97米（36英尺）；同时可标出底线中点J和距C、D点1.37米（4英尺6英寸）的单打边线c、d两点。

中线和发球线各点F、H、G均可分别在bc、 XJ、 ad线上距球网6.4米（ 21英尺 ）处画出。

采取同样步骤可画完球网另一边的球场。

如果只需要单打球场，虽然a、b、c、d外边之线均不必画，但仍可用以上方法丈量出球场。或者，也可在a、b处加钉并各与一量尺相连以代替A、B，再用14.46米（47英尺5英寸）和11.89米（39英尺）的长度，找出单打底线的两角c、d。网柱在n、n处并应使用10米（33英尺）长的单打球网。

当一个单打、双打兼用球场挂着双打球网用于单打比赛时，球网必须在n、n处用两根1.07米（3英尺6英寸）高的单打支柱撑起，单打支柱的直径或边长不得超过7.5厘米（3英寸）。单打支柱的中心应距单打场地外0.914米（3英尺）。

为了便于安置单打支柱，最好在画场地时将n、n两点用白点标出。

当执行机构同意使用“混合线”时，应遵守以下原则。

颜色：

- 使用与地面背景色同一色系的颜色。
- 颜色比地面背景色略浅。
- 色差不超过22度（即背景色增加不多于25%的白色）。

速度：

- 与地面速度相差不超过5 CPR。

尺寸：

- 比标准线窄1.0 ~ 1.5厘米。

标记：

- 与白色界线相交处有8厘米的距离。

**注：**作为国际性比赛的指导原则，底线和后挡板之间的距离不应少于6.40米（21英尺），边线和侧挡板之间的距离不应少于3.66米（12英尺）。

作为休闲和俱乐部比赛的指导原则，底线和后挡板之间的距离不应少于5.48米（18英尺），边线和侧挡板之间的距离不应少于3.05米（10英尺）。

作为一项指导原则，室内球场的天花板的最低高度（从球网处测量）建议为9.0米（29.6英尺）。

# 附录X 沙滩网球规则

沙滩网球规则由网球规则委员会及董事会批准，可以通过网站查询：https://www.itftennis.com/en/itf-tours/beach-tennis-tour/

# 附录XI　网球规则的审查与听证程序

## 1. 绪论

1.1 本程序由国际网球联合会董事会（以下简称“董事会”）于1998年5月17日审议通过。

1.2 董事会可以根据需要补充、修订或变更本程序。

## 2. 目的

2.1 国际网联是网球规则的监督者并致力于：

a. 维护网球赛事的传统和诚信。

b. 积极维护网球比赛的传统技术。

c. 鼓励发展，使比赛保持挑战性。

d. 保证公平竞争。

2.2 为了保证公平、连贯、高效地进行网球规则的审查与听证，应当采用以下的程序。

## 3. 范围

本程序适用于以下规则的裁定：

a. 第1条——场地。

b. 第3条——球。

c. 第4条 —— 球拍。

d. 网球规则附录Ⅰ和附录Ⅱ

e. 国际网联可以作出决定的其他任何有关网球规则的问题。

## 4. 结构

4.1 根据本程序规定，由裁决委员会公布裁决结果。

4.2 裁决委员会的裁决为最终裁决。但依据本程序，当事人有权向申诉庭提起申诉。

## 5. 申请

受理申诉的依据：

a. 根据董事会的提议；或

b. 根据以下程序提出的申请。

## 6. 裁决委员会的任命和组成

6.1 裁决委员会由国际网联主席（以下简称“主席”）或其指定人员任命，组成人员数量由主席或其指定人员决定。

6.2 如果有超过一人被任命组成裁决委员会，那么裁决委员会应从中提名一人担任裁决委员会主席。

6.3 裁决委员会主席有权调整裁决委员会举行任何听证会

之前和听证会过程中的程序。

## 7. 裁决委员会的拟定裁决

7.1 董事会议案中提出的所有拟作裁决细节，将通知到对该拟定判决真正感兴趣的任何人，或是运动员、器材生产厂商，或是国家网球协会或其会员。

7.2 将给予被通知人员合理的时间，使其能够向与该裁决相关的董事会主席或其指定人员提交评论、反对意见或要求获得更多信息。

## 8. 裁决的申请

8.1 任何真正感兴趣的个体，包括运动员、器材生产厂商、国家网球协会或其会员都可以对裁决提出申请。

8.2 任何裁决的申请必须以书面形式递交给董事会主席。

8.3 有效的裁决申请必须包含至少以下具体信息：

a. 申请人的全名和地址。

b. 申请日期。

c. 应清楚地阐明申请人要求解释的裁决问题。

d. 在听证中申请人所应提供的所有相关的证据文件。

e. 如果申请人认为鉴定证据是必要的，那么他可以要求在听证会中鉴定证据，但必须明确鉴定人的姓名及其相关专业。

f. 当申请的裁决是有关球拍或其他器材时，必须将涉及器材的样品或其复制品连同申请书一并递交。

g. 如果申请人有特殊或异常情况，需要在指定的时间内或日期前完成裁决，那么申请人应当详述这一特殊或异常情况。

8.4 如果裁决申请中没有包括上述8.3项中a~g条所涉及的信息或装备问题，主席或其指定人员应通知申请人，申请人应在指定的合理时间内补齐这些缺项。如果申请人不能在指定的时间内补齐这些缺项，申请将被驳回。

## 9. 召开裁决委员会会议

9.1 根据有效的申请或董事会提出的议案，裁决委员会主席或其指定人员应召开裁决会议来处理此申请或议案。

9.2 凡是裁判委员会主席认为不需要听证就可以公平处理的申请或议案，裁决委员会可不必举行听证。

## 10. 裁决委员会程序

10.1 裁决委员会主席应决定每次审查/听证的恰当形式、程序和日期。

10.2 裁决委员会主席应将上述10.1条款中的内容以书面方式告知申请人，或每一位对拟定裁决表示异议的人或协会。

10.3 裁判委员会主席应决定与证据相关的所有问题，并且不受法定议事程序和采纳证据的约束，只要审查/听证能够公平地进行，每一位相关的当事人都有合理的机会进行陈述。

10.4 任何审查/听证都应当依照如下程序进行：

a. 非公开举行。

b. 裁决委员会必要时可以暂停或延期举行。

10.5 在处理需要特殊技术或经验的特定问题时，裁判委员会主席有权决定与裁决委员会外具备特殊技术或特殊知识的附加成员进行持续合作。

10.6 裁决委员会应根据多数人的意见进行裁决。任何裁决委员会的人员都不能弃权。

10.7 裁决委员会主席有绝对的权力决定收取申请人（或其他在审查/听证中持反对意见、要求解释的个人或组织）相关的申请费用、裁决委员会进行测试所需的合理费用或为违反规则规定装备提供报告证书的合理费用。

## 11. 通知

11.1 一旦裁决委员会作出裁决，就应以书面方式在尽可能短的合理期限内通知申请人或其他任何相关的个人或协会。

11.2 书面通知应当包括裁决委员会的裁决理由。

11.3 在申请人收到裁决通知后或裁决委员会另行指定的日期过后，裁决委员会作出的裁决立即生效。

## 12. 现行网球规则的应用

12.1 尽管裁决委员会有权出台过渡性规则，在裁决委员会审查/听证结束、公布裁决之前，现行网球规则仍然适用。

12.2 在进行审查/听证之前或期间，裁决委员会主席可以提出指导性意见，作为网球规则和包括过渡性规则在内的其他规则合理必要的实施原则。

12.3 在裁决委员会没有就装备是否符合网球规则的要求作出裁决的情况下，过渡性规则可以包括限制使用这些装备的条款。

## 13. 申诉庭的任命与组成

13.1 申诉庭由主席或其指定人员从董事会成员中任命。

13.2 作出原裁决的裁决委员会成员不能成为申诉庭成员。

13.3 申诉庭的人数由主席或其指定人员决定，但应不少于3人。

13.4 申诉庭应提名一名成员担任申诉庭主席。

13.5 申诉庭主席有权调整申诉听证会之前或期间的程序。

## 14. 提出申诉

14.1 申请人（或任何对拟裁决提出意见、异议或要求的有关个人或组织）可以对裁决委员会的任何裁决提出申诉。

14.2 有效申诉必须符合以下情况：

a. 收到裁决通知书后45天内，以书面形式向作出裁决的裁决委员会主席提起申诉。

b. 必须详细陈述申诉的内容。

c. 必须包括申诉的所有理由。

14.3 作为申诉条件，在作出原裁决的裁决委员会主席收到有效申诉时，可以要求申诉人支付一定数额的申诉费。如果申诉成功，该申诉费应当退还申诉人。

## 15. 召开申诉庭会议

15.1 申诉人缴纳申诉费后，主席或其指定人员应召开申诉庭会议。

## 16. 申诉庭的程序

16.1 申诉庭及其主席应根据前面第10、11和12条的规定执行程序和举行听证会。

16.2 根据网球竞赛规则，在申诉人收到通知或申诉庭确定的日期过后，申诉庭的裁决为最终裁决并立即生效。

## 17. 原则

17.1 如果裁决委员会只有一人，那么该成员作为主席负责管理听证会并决定听证会举行之前和期间应当遵守的程序。

17.2 所有审查/听证使用的语言为英语。如果申诉人、持反对意见或要求解释的其他个人或组织不懂英语，则必须有翻译人员在场。翻译人员必须尽可能保持中立。

17.3 裁决委员会或申诉庭可以公布裁决摘要。

17.4 按本程序规定，所有通知书均应采用书面形式。

17.5 所有按本程序规定告知、寄送或传送给申请人或其他相关人员通知之日，即视为已经完成通知。

17.6 如果裁决委员会合理认定某一申请与已经作出决定或裁决的申请或提议大体相同，并且裁决是在此次申请日期之前的36个月之内作出的，那么裁决委员会有权不予受理。

# 2023年规则变化

为了对网球竞赛规则的潜在变化进行试验，相关部门可以申请在特定期限内或特定赛事中更改本规则。网球竞赛规则委员会将慎重考虑相关申请，申请通过后将提交国际网球联合会董事会正式批准。

以下对网球竞赛规则的临时变更是于2020年、2021年和2022年最初由国际网球联合会董事会批准，由于新型冠状病毒大流行导致2021年举办的赛事数量有限，因此经与申请方商议，这些临时变更延长至2023年。

**规则2——永久固定物：**

•获得国际网球联合会运动员分析技术（PAT）设备许可的公司可以将PAT装置附着于网柱上，用于界线判罚和运动员分析。

**规则30——指导：**

•在WTA、ATP和大满贯赛事中可以试行场外指导。

**附录Ⅴ——备选程序和计分方法：**

•大满贯赛事可以试行在男子、女子单打和双打比赛中，当决胜盘比分达到6：6时使用一个十分制平局决胜局决定比赛胜负，包括大满贯的轮椅单打、双打比赛和青少年单打比赛。

**沙滩网球规则附录Ⅲ——球：**

•沙滩网球巡回赛可以使用2阶网球代替规则中原定的颜

色规格（如蓝色和黄色、紫色和黄色、紫色和橙色、紫色和绿色）。

**附录Ⅶ——10岁及以下年龄组的网球比赛：**

• 在10岁及以下年龄组的网球比赛中可以使用以下高度的球网：

• 在红球场地上，球网中心的高度为0.600米（23.6英寸）至0.650米（25.6英寸）。

• 在橙球场地上，球网中心的高度为0.650米（25.6英寸）至0.700米（27.6英寸）。

• 在绿球场地上，即规则1中描述的（全尺寸）场地，球网中心的高度为0.700米（27.6英寸）至0.800米（31.5英寸）。

在规则试行期间，在10岁及以下年龄组三种类型的网球比赛中，各国家协会在上述规定的范围内有权决定球网中心的高度。

在试行阶段结束后，申请方应向网球竞赛规则委员会提交一份报告。

网球竞赛规则委员会由大满贯、ATP、WTA和国际网球联合会国家网球协会的相关代表组成。

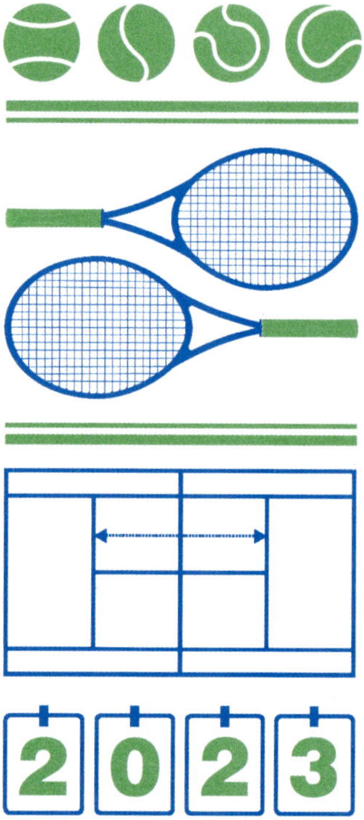


# ITF RULES OF TENNIS

ITF
International Tennis Federation

# CONTENTS

*References to the International Tennis Federation or ITF shall hereafter mean ITF Limited.*

# FOREWORD

The International Tennis Federation (ITF) is the governing body of the game of tennis and its duties and responsibilities include protecting the integrity of the game through determination of the Rules of Tennis.

To assist the ITF in carrying out this responsibility, the ITF has appointed a Rules of Tennis Committee which continually monitors the game and its rules, and when considered necessary makes recommendations for changes to the Board of Directors of the ITF who in turn make recommendations to the Annual General Meeting of the ITF which is the ultimate authority for making any changes to the Rules of Tennis.

Appendix V lists approved alternative procedures and scoring methods. In addition, on its own behalf or on application by interested parties, certain variations to the rules may be approved by the ITF for trial purposes only at a limited number of tournaments or events and/or for a limited time period. Such variations are not included in the published rules and require a report to the ITF on the conclusion of the approved trial.

---

*Note: If there are any inconsistencies between the English version and Rules of Tennis translated into other languages, the English version shall prevail.*

# RULES OF TENNIS

## 1. THE COURT

The court shall be a rectangle, 78 feet (23.77 m) long and, for singles matches, 27 feet (8.23 m) wide. For doubles matches, the court shall be 36 feet (10.97 m) wide.

The court shall be divided across the middle by a net suspended by a cord or metal cable which shall pass over or be attached to two net posts at a height of 3 ½ feet (1.07 m). The net shall be fully extended so that it completely fills the space between the two net posts and it must be of sufficiently small mesh to ensure that a ball cannot pass through it. The height of the net shall be 3 feet (0.914 m) at the centre, where it shall be held down tightly by a strap. A band shall cover the cord or metal cable and the top of the net. The strap and band shall be completely white.

- The maximum diameter of the cord or metal cable shall be 1/3 inch (0.8 cm).
- The maximum width of the strap shall be 2 inches (5 cm).
- The band shall be between 2 inches (5 cm) and 2 ½ inches (6.35 cm) deep on each side.

For doubles matches, the centres of the net posts shall be 3 feet (0.914 m) outside the doubles court on each side.

For singles matches, if a singles net is used, the centres of the net posts shall be 3 feet (0.914 m) outside the singles court on each side. If a doubles net is used, then the net shall be supported, at a height of 3 1/2 feet (1.07 m), by two singles sticks, the centres of which shall be 3 feet (0.914 m) outside the singles court on each side.

- The net posts shall not be more than 6 inches (15 cm) square or 6 inches (15 cm) in diameter.
- The singles sticks shall not be more than 3 inches (7.5 cm) square or 3 inches (7.5 cm) in diameter.
- The net posts and singles sticks shall not be more than 1 inch (2.5 cm) above the top of the net cord.

The lines at the ends of the court are called baselines and the lines at the sides of the court are called sidelines.

Two lines shall be drawn between the singles sidelines, 21 feet (6.40 m) from each side of the net, parallel with the net. These lines are called the servicelines. On each side of the net, the area between the serviceline and the net shall be divided into two equal parts, the service courts, by the centre serviceline. The centre serviceline shall be drawn parallel with the singles sidelines and half-way between them.

Each baseline shall be divided in half by a centre mark, 4 inches (10 cm) in length, which shall be drawn inside the court and parallel with the singles sidelines.

- The centre serviceline and centre mark shall be 2 inches (5 cm) wide.

- The other lines of the court shall be between 1 inch (2.5 cm) and 2 inches (5 cm) wide, except that the baselines may be up to 4 inches (10 cm) wide.

All court measurements shall be made to the outside of the lines and all lines of the court shall be of the same colour clearly contrasting with the colour of the surface.

No advertising is allowed on the court, net, strap, band, net posts or singles sticks except as provided in Appendix IV.

In addition to the court described above, the court designated as "Red" and the court designated as "Orange" in Appendix VII can be used for 10 and under tennis competition.

*Note: Guidelines for minimum distances between the baseline and backstops and between the sidelines and sidestops can be found in Appendix IX.*

## 2. PERMANENT FIXTURES

The permanent fixtures of the court include the backstops and sidestops, the spectators, the stands and seats for spectators, all other fixtures around and above the court, the chair umpire, line umpires, net umpire and ball persons when in their recognised positions.

In a singles match played with a doubles net and singles sticks, the net posts and the part of the net outside the singles sticks are permanent fixtures and are not considered as net posts or part of the net.

## 3. THE BALL

Balls, which are approved for play under the Rules of Tennis, must comply with the specifications in Appendix I.

The International Tennis Federation shall rule on the question of whether any ball or prototype complies with Appendix I or is otherwise approved, or not approved, for play. Such ruling may be taken on its own initiative or upon application by any party with a bona fide interest therein, including any player, equipment manufacturer or National Association or members thereof. Such rulings and applications shall be made in accordance with the applicable Review and Hearing Procedures of the International Tennis Federation (see Appendix XI).

The event organisers must announce in advance of the event:

a. The number of balls for play (2, 3, 4 or 6).

b. The ball change policy, if any.

Ball changes, if any, can be made either:

i. After an agreed odd number of games, in which case, the first ball change in the match shall take place two games earlier than for the rest of the match, to make allowance for the warm-up. A tie-break game counts as one game for the ball change. A ball change shall not take place at the beginning of a tie-break game. In this case, the ball change shall be delayed until the beginning of the second game of the next set; or

ii. At the beginning of a set.

If a ball gets broken during play, the point shall be replayed.

*Case 1: If a ball is soft at the end of a point, should the point be replayed?*

*Decision: If the ball is soft, not broken, the point shall not be replayed.*

*Note: Any ball to be used in a tournament which is played under the Rules of Tennis must be named on the official ITF list of approved balls issued by the International Tennis Federation.*

## 4. THE RACKET

Rackets, which are approved for play under the Rules of Tennis, must comply with the specifications in Appendix II.

The International Tennis Federation shall rule on the question of whether any racket or prototype complies with Appendix II or is otherwise approved, or not approved, for play. Such ruling may be undertaken on its own initiative or upon application by any party with a bona fide interest therein, including any player, equipment manufacturer or National Association or members thereof. Such rulings and applications shall be made in accordance with the applicable Review and Hearing Procedures of the International Tennis Federation (see Appendix XI).

*Case 1: Is more than one set of strings allowed on the hitting surface of a racket?*

Decision: *No. The rule mentions a pattern (not patterns) of crossed strings (See Appendix II).*

Case 2: *Is the stringing pattern of a racket considered to be generally uniform and flat if the strings are on more than one plane?*

Decision: *No.*

Case 3: *Can vibration damping devices be placed on the strings of a racket? If so, where can they be placed?*

Decision: *Yes, but these devices may only be placed outside the pattern of the crossed strings.*

Case 4: *During a point, a player accidentally breaks the strings. Can the player continue to play another point with this racket?*

Decision: *Yes, except where specifically prohibited by event organisers.*

Case 5: *Is a player allowed to use more than one racket at any time during play?*

Decision: *No.*

Case 6: *Can a battery that affects playing characteristics be incorporated into a racket?*

Decision: *No. A battery is prohibited because it is an energy source, as are solar cells and other similar devices.*

## 5. SCORE IN A GAME

a. Standard game

A standard game is scored as follows with the server's score being called first:

| | | |
|---|---|---|
| No point | — | "Love" |
| First point | — | "15" |
| Second point | — | "30" |
| Third point | — | "40" |
| Fourth point | — | "Game" |

except that if each player/team has won three points, the score is "Deuce". After "Deuce", the score is "Advantage" for the player/team who wins the next point. If that same player/team also wins the next point, that player/team wins the "Game"; if the opposing player/team wins the next point, the score is again "Deuce". A player/team needs to win two consecutive points immediately after "Deuce" to win the "Game".

b. Tie-break game

During a tie-break game, points are scored "Zero", "1", "2", "3", etc. The first player/team to win seven points wins the "Game" and "Set", provided there is a margin of two points over the opponent(s). If necessary, the tie-break game shall continue until this margin is achieved.

The player whose turn it is to serve shall serve the first point of the tie-break game. The following two points shall be served by the opponent(s) (in doubles, the player of the opposing team due to serve next). After this, each player/team shall serve alternately for two consecutive points until the end of the tie-break game (in doubles, the rotation of service within each team shall continue in the same order as during that set).

The player/team whose turn it was to serve first in the tie-break game shall be the receiver in the first game of the following set.

Additional approved alternative scoring methods can be found in Appendix V.

## 6. SCORE IN A SET

There are different methods of scoring in a set. The two main methods are the "Advantage Set" and the "Tie-break Set". Either method may be used provided that the one to be used is announced in advance of the event. If the "Tie-break Set" method is to be used, it must also be announced whether the final set will be played as a "Tie-break Set" or an "Advantage Set".

a. "Advantage Set"

The first player/team to win six games wins that "Set", provided there is a margin of two games over the opponent(s). If necessary, the set shall continue until this margin is achieved.

b. "Tie-break Set"

The first player/team to win six games wins that "Set", provided there is a margin of two games over the opponent(s). If the score reaches six games all, a tie-break game shall be played.

Additional approved alternative scoring methods can be found in Appendix V.

## 7. SCORE IN A MATCH

A match can be played to the best of 3 sets (a player/team needs to win 2 sets to win the match) or to the best of 5 sets (a player/team needs to win 3 sets to win the match).

Additional approved alternative scoring methods can be found in Appendix V.

## 8. SERVER AND RECEIVER

The players/teams shall stand on opposite sides of the net. The server is the player who puts the ball into play for the first point. The receiver is the player who is ready to return the ball served by the server.

*Case 1: Is the receiver allowed to stand outside the lines of the court?*

*Decision: Yes. The receiver may take any position inside or outside the lines on the receiver's side of the net.*

## 9. CHOICE OF ENDS AND SERVICE

The choice of ends and the choice to be server or receiver in the first game shall be decided by toss before the warm-up starts. The player/team who wins the toss may choose:

a. To be server or receiver in the first game of the match, in which case the opponent(s) shall choose the end of the court for the first game of the match; or

b. The end of the court for the first game of the match, in which case the opponent(s) shall choose to be server or receiver for the first game of the match; or

c. To require the opponent(s) to make one of the above choices.

*Case 1: Do both players/teams have the right to new choices if the warm-up is stopped and the players leave the court?*

*Decision: Yes. The result of the original toss stands, but new choices may be made by both players/teams.*

## 10. CHANGE OF ENDS

The players shall change ends at the end of the first, third and every subsequent odd game of each set. The players shall also change ends at the end of each set unless the total number of games in that set is even, in which case the players change ends at the end of the first game of the next set.

During a tie-break game, players shall change ends after every six points.

Additional approved alternative procedures can be found in Appendix V.

## 11. BALL IN PLAY

Unless a fault or a let is called, the ball is in play from the moment the server hits the ball, and remains in play until the point is decided.

## 12. BALL TOUCHES A LINE

If a ball touches a line, it is regarded as touching the court bounded by that line.

## 13. BALL TOUCHES A PERMANENT FIXTURE

If the ball in play touches a permanent fixture after it has hit the correct court, the player who hit the ball wins the point. If the ball in play touches a permanent fixture before it hits the ground, the player who hit the ball loses the point.

## 14. ORDER OF SERVICE

At the end of each standard game, the receiver shall become the server and the server shall become the receiver for the next game.
In doubles, the team due to serve in the first game of each set shall decide which player shall serve for that game. Similarly, before the

second game starts, their opponents shall decide which player shall serve for that game. The partner of the player who served in the first game shall serve in the third game and the partner of the player who served in the second game shall serve in the fourth game. This rotation shall continue until the end of the set.

## 15. ORDER OF RECEIVING IN DOUBLES

The team which is due to receive in the first game of a set shall decide which player shall receive the first point in the game. Similarly, before the second game starts, their opponents shall decide which player shall receive the first point of that game. The player who was the receiver's partner for the first point of the game shall receive the second point and this rotation shall continue until the end of the game and the set. After the receiver has returned the ball, either player in a team can hit the ball.

*Case 1: Is one member of a doubles team allowed to play alone against the opponents?*

*Decision: No.*

## 16. THE SERVICE

Immediately before starting the service motion, the server shall stand at rest with both feet behind (i.e. further from the net than) the baseline and within the imaginary extensions of the centre mark and the sideline.

The server shall then release the ball by hand in any direction and hit the ball with the racket before the ball hits the ground. The service motion is completed at the moment that the player's racket hits or misses the ball. A player who is able to use only one arm may use the racket for the release of the ball.

## 17. SERVING

When serving in a standard game, the server shall stand behind alternate halves of the court, starting from the right half of the court in every game.

In a tie-break game, the service shall be served from behind alternate halves of the court, with the first served from the right half of the court.

The service shall pass over the net and hit the service court diagonally opposite, before the receiver returns it.

## 18. FOOT FAULT

During the service motion, the server shall not:

a. Change position by walking or running, although slight movements of the feet are permitted; or

b. Touch the baseline or the court with either foot; or

c. Touch the area outside the imaginary extension of the sideline with either foot; or

d. Touch the imaginary extension of the centre mark with either foot.

If the server breaks this rule it is a "Foot Fault".

*Case 1: In a singles match, is the server allowed to serve standing behind the part of the baseline between the singles sideline and the doubles sideline?*

*Decision: No.*

*Case 2: Is the server allowed to have one or both feet off the ground?*

*Decision: Yes.*

## 19. SERVICE FAULT

The service is a fault if:

a. The server breaks Rules 16, 17 or 18; or

b. The server misses the ball when trying to hit it; or

c. The ball served touches a permanent fixture, singles stick or net post before it hits the ground; or

d. The ball served touches the server or server's partner, or anything the server or server's partner is wearing or carrying.

*Case 1: After tossing a ball to serve, the server decides not to hit it and catches it instead. Is this a fault?*

*Decision: No. A player, who tosses the ball and then decides not to hit it, is allowed to catch the ball with the hand or the racket, or to let the ball bounce.*

*Case 2: During a singles match played on a court with net posts and singles sticks, the ball served hits a singles stick and then hits the correct service court. Is this a fault?*

*Decision: Yes.*

## 20. SECOND SERVICE

If the first service is a fault, the server shall serve again without delay from behind the same half of the court from which that fault was served, unless the service was from the wrong half.

## 21. WHEN TO SERVE AND RECEIVE

The server shall not serve until the receiver is ready. However, the receiver shall play to the reasonable pace of the server and shall be ready to receive within a reasonable time of the server being ready. A receiver who attempts to return the service shall be considered as being ready. If it is demonstrated that the receiver is not ready, the service cannot be called a fault.

## 22. THE LET DURING A SERVICE

The service is a let if:

a. The ball served touches the net, strap or band, and is otherwise good; or, after touching the net, strap or band, touches the receiver or the receiver's partner or anything they wear or carry before hitting the ground; or

b. The ball is served when the receiver is not ready.

In the case of a service let, that particular service shall not count, and the server shall serve again, but a service let does not cancel a previous fault.

Additional approved alternative procedures can be found in Appendix V.

## 23. THE LET

In all cases when a let is called, except when a service let is called on a second service, the whole point shall be replayed.

*Case 1: When the ball is in play, another ball rolls onto court. A let is called. The server had previously served a fault. Is the server now entitled to a first service or second service?*

*Decision: First service. The whole point must be replayed.*

## 24. PLAYER LOSES POINT

The point is lost if:

a. The player serves two consecutive faults; or

b. The player does not return the ball in play before it bounces twice consecutively; or

c. The player returns the ball in play so that it hits the ground, or before it bounces, an object, outside the correct court; or

d. The player returns the ball in play so that, before it bounces, it hits a permanent fixture; or

e. The receiver returns the service before it bounces; or

f. The player deliberately carries or catches the ball in play on the racket or deliberately touches it with the racket more than once; or

g. The player or the racket, whether in the player's hand or not, or anything which the player is wearing or carrying touches the net, net posts/singles sticks, cord or metal cable, strap or band, or the opponent's court at any time while the ball is in play; or

h. The player hits the ball before it has passed the net; or

i. The ball in play touches the player or anything that the player is wearing or carrying, except the racket; or

j. The ball in play touches the racket when the player is not holding it; or

k. The player deliberately and materially changes the shape of the racket when the ball is in play; or

l. In doubles, both players touch the ball when returning it.

*Case 1: After the server has served a first service, the racket falls out of the server's hand and touches the net before the ball has bounced. Is this a service fault, or does the server lose the point?*

*Decision: The server loses the point because the racket touches the net while the ball is in play.*

Case 2: *After the server has served a first service, the racket falls out of the server's hand and touches the net after the ball has bounced outside the correct service court. Is this a service fault, or does the server lose the point?*

Decision: *This is a service fault because when the racket touched the net the ball was no longer in play.*

Case 3: *In a doubles match, the receiver's partner touches the net before the ball that has been served touches the ground outside the correct service court. What is the correct decision?*

Decision: *The receiving team loses the point because the receiver's partner touched the net while the ball was in play.*

Case 4: *Does a player lose the point if an imaginary line in the extension of the net is crossed before or after hitting the ball?*

Decision: *The player does not lose the point in either case provided the player does not touch the opponent's court.*

Case 5: *Is a player allowed to jump over the net into the opponent's court while the ball is in play?*

Decision: *No. The player loses the point.*

Case 6: *A player throws the racket at the ball in play. Both the racket and the ball land in the court on the opponent's side of the net and the opponent(s) is unable to reach the ball. Which player wins the point?*

Decision: *The player who threw the racket at the ball loses the point.*

Case 7: *A ball that has just been served hits the receiver or in doubles the receiver's partner before it touches the ground. Which player wins the point?*

Decision: *The server wins the point, unless it is a service let.*

Case 8: *A player standing outside the court hits the ball or catches it before it bounces and claims the point because the ball was definitely going out of the correct court.*

Decision: *The player loses the point, unless it is a good return, in which case the point continues.*

## 25. A GOOD RETURN

It is a good return if:

a. The ball touches the net, net posts/singles sticks, cord or metal cable, strap or band, provided that it passes over any of them and hits the ground within the correct court; except as provided in Rules 2 and 24 (d); or

b. After the ball in play has hit the ground within the correct court and has spun or been blown back over the net, the player reaches over the net and plays the ball into the correct court, provided that the player does not break Rule 24; or

c. The ball is returned outside the net posts, either above or below the level of the top of the net, even though it touches the net posts, provided that it hits the ground in the correct court; except as provided in Rules 2 and 24 (d); or

d. The ball passes under the net cord between the singles stick and the adjacent net post without touching either net, net cord or net post and hits the ground in the correct court, or

e. The player's racket passes over the net after hitting the ball on the player's own side of the net and the ball hits the ground in the correct court; or

f. The player hits the ball in play, which hits another ball lying in the correct court.

*Case 1: A player returns a ball which then hits a singles stick and hits the ground in the correct court. Is this a good return?*

*Decision: Yes. However, if the ball is served and hits the singles stick, it is a service fault.*

*Case 2: A ball in play hits another ball which is lying in the correct court. What is the correct decision?*

*Decision: Play continues. However, if it is not clear that the actual ball in play has been returned, a let should be called.*

## 26. HINDRANCE

If a player is hindered in playing the point by a deliberate act of the opponent(s), the player shall win the point.

However, the point shall be replayed if a player is hindered in playing the point by either an unintentional act of the opponent(s), or something outside the player's own control (not including a permanent fixture).

*Case 1: Is an unintentional double hit a hindrance?*

*Decision:* *No. See also Rule 24 (f).*

*Case 2:* *A player claims to have stopped play because the player thought that the opponent(s) was being hindered. Is this a hindrance?*

*Decision:* *No, the player loses the point.*

*Case 3:* *A ball in play hits a bird flying over the court. Is this a hindrance?*

*Decision:* *Yes, the point shall be replayed.*

*Case 4:* *During a point, a ball or other object that was lying on the player's side of the net when the point started hinders the player. Is this a hindrance?*

*Decision:* *No.*

*Case 5:* *In doubles, where are the server's partner and receiver's partner allowed to stand?*

*Decision:* *The server's partner and the receiver's partner may take any position on their own side of the net, inside or outside the court. However, if a player is creating a hindrance to the opponent(s), the hindrance rule should be used.*

## 27. CORRECTING ERRORS

As a principle, when an error in respect of the Rules of Tennis is discovered, all points previously played shall stand. Errors so discovered shall be corrected as follows:

a. During a standard game or a tie-break game, if a player serves from the wrong half of the court, this should be corrected as soon as the error is discovered and the server shall serve from the correct half of the court according to the score. A fault that was served before the error was discovered shall stand.

b. During a standard game or a tie-break game, if the players are at the wrong ends of the court, the error should be corrected as soon as it is discovered and the server shall serve from the correct end of the court according to the score.

c. If a player serves out of turn during a standard game, the player who was originally due to serve shall serve as soon as the error is discovered. However, if a game is completed before the error is discovered the order of service shall remain as altered. In this case, any ball change to be made after an agreed number of games should be made one game later than originally scheduled. A fault that was served by the opponents(s) before the error was discovered shall not stand.

In doubles, if the partners of one team serve out of turn, a fault that was served before the error was discovered shall stand.

d. If a player serves out of turn during a tie-break game and the error is discovered after an even number of points have been played, the error is corrected immediately. If the error is discovered after an odd number of points have been played, the order of service shall remain as altered.

A fault that was served by the opponent(s) before the error was discovered shall not stand.

In doubles, if the partners of one team serve out of turn, a fault that was served before the error was discovered shall stand.

e. During a standard game or a tie-break game in doubles, if there is an error in the order of receiving, this shall remain as altered until the end of the game in which the error is discovered. For the next game in which they are the receivers in that set, the partners shall then resume the original order of receiving.

f. If in error a tie-break game is started at 6 games all, when it was previously agreed that the set would be an "Advantage set", the error shall be corrected immediately if only one point has been played. If the error is discovered after the second point is in play, the set will continue as a "Tie-break set".

g. If in error a standard game is started at 6 games all, when it was previously agreed that the set would be a "Tie-break set", the error shall be corrected immediately if only one point has been played. If the error is discovered after the second point is in play, the set will continue as an "Advantage set" until the score reaches 8 games all (or a higher even number), when a tie-break game shall be played.

h. If in error an "Advantage set" or "Tie-break set" is started, when it was previously agreed that the final set would be a match tie-break, the error shall be corrected immediately if only one point has been played. If the error is discovered after the second point is in play, the set will continue either until a player or team wins three games (and therefore the set) or until the score reaches 2 games all, when a match tie-break shall be played. However, if the error is discovered after the second point of the fifth game has started, the set will continue as a "Tie-break set" (See Appendix V).

i. If the balls are not changed in the correct sequence, the error shall be corrected when the player/team who should have served with new balls is next due to serve a new game. Thereafter the balls shall be changed so that the number of games between ball changes shall be that originally agreed. Balls should not be changed during a game.

## 28. ROLE OF COURT OFFICIALS

For matches where officials are appointed, their roles and responsibilities can be found in Appendix VI

## 29. CONTINUOUS PLAY

As a principle, play should be continuous, from the time the match starts (when the first service of the match is put in play) until the match finishes.

a. Between points, a maximum of twenty-five (25) seconds is allowed. When the players change ends at the end of a game, a maximum of ninety (90) seconds are allowed. However, after the first game of each set and during a tie-break game, play shall be continuous and the players shall change ends without a rest.

At the end of each set there shall be a set break of a maximum of one hundred and twenty (120) seconds.

The maximum time starts from the moment that one point finishes until the first service is struck for the next point.

Event organisers may apply for ITF approval to extend the ninety (90) seconds allowed when the players change ends at the end of a game and the one hundred and twenty (120) seconds allowed at a set break.

b. If, for reasons outside the player's control, clothing, footwear or necessary equipment (excluding the racket) is broken or needs to be replaced, the player may be allowed reasonable extra time to rectify the problem.

c. No extra time shall be given to allow a player to recover condition. However, a player suffering from a treatable medical condition may be allowed one medical time-out of three minutes for the treatment of that medical condition. A limited number of toilet/change of attire breaks may also be allowed, if this is announced in advance of the event.

d. Event organisers may allow a rest period of a maximum of ten (10) minutes if this is announced in advance of the event. This rest period can be taken after the 3rd set in a best of 5 sets match, or after the 2nd set in a best of 3 sets match.

e. The warm-up time shall be a maximum of five (5) minutes,

unless otherwise decided by the event organisers.

## 30. COACHING

Coaching is considered to be communication, advice or instruction of any kind and by any means to a player.

In team events where there is a team captain sitting on-court, the team captain may coach the player(s) during a set break and when the players change ends at the end of a game, but not when the players change ends after the first game of each set and not during a tie-break game.

In all other matches, coaching is not allowed.

*Case 1: Is a player allowed to be coached, if the coaching is given by signals in a discreet way?*

*Decision: No.*

*Case 2: Is a player allowed to receive coaching when play is suspended?*

*Decision: Yes.*

*Case 3: Is a player allowed to receive on-court coaching during a match?*

*Decision: Sanctioning bodies may apply to the ITF to have on-court coaching allowed. In events where on-court coaching is allowed, designated coaches may enter the court and coach their players under procedures decided by the sanctioning body.*

## 31. PLAYER ANALYSIS TECHNOLOGY

Player analysis technology, that is approved for play under the Rules of Tennis, must comply with the specifications in Appendix III.

The International Tennis Federation shall rule on the question of whether any such equipment is approved, or not approved. Such ruling may be taken on its own initiative, or upon application by any party with a bona fide interest therein, including any player, equipment manufacturer or National Association or members thereof. Such rulings and applications shall be made in accordance with the applicable Review and Hearing Procedures of the International Tennis Federation (see Appendix XI).

# RULES OF WHEELCHAIR TENNIS

The game of wheelchair tennis follows the ITF Rules of Tennis with the following exceptions:

a. The Two Bounce Rule

The wheelchair tennis player is allowed two bounces of the ball. The player must return the ball before it bounces a third time. The second bounce can be either in or out of the court boundaries.

b. The Wheelchair

The wheelchair is considered part of the body and all applicable rules, which apply to a player's body, shall apply to the wheelchair.

c. The Service

The service shall be delivered in the following manner:

i. Immediately before commencing the service, the server shall be in a stationary position. The server shall then be allowed one push before striking the ball.

ii. The server shall throughout the delivery of the service not touch with any wheel, any area other than that behind the baseline within the imaginary extension of the centre mark and sideline.

iii. If conventional methods for the service are physically impossible for a quad player, then the player or another individual may drop the ball for such a player and allow it to bounce before it is struck. If this is the case, the same method of serving must be used for the entire match.

d. Player Loses Point

A player loses a point if:

i. The player fails to return the ball before it has bounced three times; or

ii. Subject to (Rule f) below the player uses any part of their feet or lower extremities against the ground or against any wheel while delivering service, striking a ball, turning or stopping while the ball is in play; or

iii. The player fails to keep one buttock in contact with their wheelchair seat when contacting the ball.

e. The Wheelchair

Wheelchairs used in all competitions played under the Rules of Wheelchair Tennis must comply with the following specifications:

i. The wheelchair may be constructed of any material provided that such material is non-reflective and does not constitute a hindrance to the opponent.

ii. Wheels may have a single pushrim only. No changes to the wheelchair that afford the player a mechanical advantage are permitted, such as levers or gears. During normal play, wheels shall not leave permanent marks on, or otherwise damage, the court surface.

iii. Subject to Rule e(v), players shall use only the wheels (including pushrims) to propel the wheelchair. No steering, braking or gearing or other device that may assist operation of the wheelchair, including energy storage systems, is permitted.

iv. The height of the seat (including cushion) shall be fixed and players' buttocks shall remain in contact with the seat during the playing of a point. Strapping may be used to secure the player to the wheelchair.

v. Players who meet the requirements of Article 10 of the ITF Wheelchair Tennis Classification Rules may use a wheelchair powered by electric motor(s) (a "powered wheelchair"). Powered wheelchairs must not be able to exceed 15 km/h in any direction and shall be controlled by the player only.

vi. Applications may be made for modifications to the wheelchair for legitimate medical reasons. All such applications shall be submitted to the ITF Sport Science & Medicine Commission for approval a minimum of 60 days prior to intended use in an ITF-sanctioned event. A decision to reject a proposed modification may be appealed under Chapter III of the ITF Wheelchair Tennis Regulations.

f. Propelling the Chair with the Foot

i. If due to lack of capacity a player is unable to propel the wheelchair via the wheel then they may propel the wheelchair using one foot.

ii. Even if in accordance with Rule f (i.) above a player is permitted to propel the chair using one foot, no part of the player's foot may be in contact with the ground:

a) during the forward motion of the swing, including when the racket strikes the ball;

b) from the initiation of the service motion until the racket strikes the ball.

iii. A player in breach of this rule shall lose the point.

g. Wheelchair/Able-bodied Tennis

Where a wheelchair tennis player is playing with or against an able-bodied person in singles or doubles, the Rules of Wheelchair Tennis shall apply for the wheelchair player while the Rules of Tennis for able-bodied tennis shall apply for the able-bodied player. In this instance, the wheelchair player is allowed two bounces while the able-bodied player is allowed only one bounce.

*Note: The definition of lower extremities is: the lower limbs, including the buttocks, hips, thighs, legs, ankles and feet.*

# AMENDMENT TO THE RULES OF TENNIS

(Article 28 of the Constitution of ITF Ltd)

The official and decisive text to the Rules of Tennis shall be for ever in the English language and no alteration or interpretation of such Rules shall be made except at an Annual General Meeting of the Council, nor unless notice of the Resolution embodying such alterations shall have been received by the ITF in accordance with Article 17 and such Resolution or one having the like effect shall be carried by a majority of two-thirds of the votes recorded in respect of the same.

Any alteration so made shall take effect as from the first day of January following, unless the Meeting shall by the like majority decide otherwise.

The Board of Directors shall have power, however, to settle all urgent questions of interpretation subject to confirmation at the General Meeting next following.

This text shall not be altered at any time without the unanimous consent of a General Meeting of the Council.

# APPENDIX

## APPENDIX Ⅰ THE BALL

For all measurements in Appendix I, SI units shall take precedence.

a. The ball shall have a uniform outer surface consisting of a fabric cover except for the Stage 3 (Red) foam ball. If there are any seams they shall be stitchless.

b. The ball shall conform to one of types specified in the table immediately below or in the table under paragraph (d).

| | TYPE 1 (FAST) | TYPE 2 (MEDIUM)[1] | TYPE 3 (SLOW)[2] | HIGH ALTITUDE[3] |
|---|---|---|---|---|
| MASS (WEIGHT) | 56.0–59.4 grams (1.975–2.095 ounces) | 56.0–59.4 grams (1.975–2.095 ounces) | 56.0–59.4 grams (1.975–2.095 ounces) | 56.0–59.4 grams (1.975–2.095 ounces) |
| SIZE | 6.54–6.86 cm (2.57–2.70 inches) | 6.54–6.86 cm (2.57–2.70 inches) | 7.00–7.30 cm (2.76–2.87 inches) | 6.54–6.86 cm (2.57–2.70 inches) |
| REBOUND | 138–151cm (54–60 inches) | 135–147cm (53–58 inches) | 135–147cm (53–58 inches) | 122–135 cm (48–53inches) |
| FORWARD DEFORMATION[4] | 0.56–0.74 cm (0.220–0.291 inches) | 0.56–0.74 cm (0.220–0.291 inches) | 0.56–0.74 cm (0.220–0.291 inches) | 0.56–0.74cm (0.220–0.291 inches) |
| RETURN DEFORMATION[4] | 0.74–1.08 cm (0.291–0.425 inches) | 0.80–1.08 cm (0.315–0.425 inches) | 0.80–1.08 cm (0.315–0.425 inches) | 0.80–1.08 cm (0.315–0.425 inches) |
| COLOUR | White or Yellow | White or Yellow | White or Yellow | White or Yellow |

Notes:

[1] This ball type may be pressurised or pressureless. The pressureless ball shall have an internal pressure that is no greater than 7 kPa (1 psi) and may be used for high altitude play above 1,219 m (4,000 feet) above sea level and shall have been acclimatised for 60 days or more at the altitude of the specific tournament.

[2] This ball type is also recommended for high altitude play on any court surface type above 1,219 m (4,000 feet) above sea level.

[3] This ball type is pressurised and is specified for high altitude play above 1,219 m (4,000 feet) above sea level only.

[4] The deformation shall be the average of a single reading along each of three perpendicular axes. No two individual readings shall differ by more than 0.08 cm (0.031 inches).

c. In addition, all ball types specified under paragraph (b) shall conform to the requirements for durability as shown in the following table:

| | MASS (WEIGHT) | REBOUND | FORWARD DEFORMATION | RETURN DEFORMATION |
|---|---|---|---|---|
| MAXIMUM CHANGE[1] | 0.4 grams (0.014 ounces) | 4.0 cm (1.6 inches) | 0.08 cm (0.031 inches) | 0.10 cm (0.039 inches) |

Notes:

[1] The largest permissible change in the specified properties resulting from the durability test described in the current edition of *ITF Approved Tennis Balls, Classified Surfaces & Recognised Courts*. The durability test uses laboratory equipment to simulate the effects of nine games of play.

d. Only the ball types specified in the table below can be used in 10 and under tennis competition:

| | STAGE 3 (RED) FOAM | STAGE 3 (RED) STANDARD | STAGE 2 (ORANGE) STANDARD | STAGE 1 (GREEN) STANDARD |
|---|---|---|---|---|
| MASS (WEIGHT) | 25.0–43.0 grams (0.882–1.517 ounces) | 36.0–49.0 grams (1.270–1.728 ounces) | 36.0–46.9 grams (1.270–1.654 ounces) | 47.0–51.5 grams (1.658–1.817 ounces) |
| SIZE | 8.00–9.00 cm (3.15–3.54 inches) | 7.00–8.00 cm (2.76–3.15 inches) | 6.00–6.86 cm (2.36–2.70 inches) | 6.30–6.86 cm (2.48–2.70 inches) |
| REBOUND | 85–105 cm (33–41 inches) | 90–105 cm (35–41 inches) | 105–120 cm (41–47 inches) | 120–135 cm (47–53 inches) |
| FORWARD DEFORMATION[1] | — | — | 1.40–1.65 cm (0.551–0.650 inches) | 0.80–1.05 cm (0.315–0.413 inches) |
| COLOUR[2] | Any | Red and Yellow, or Yellow with a Red dot | Orange and Yellow, or Yellow with an Orange dot | Yellow with a Green dot |

## Notes:

[1] The deformation shall be the average of a single reading along each of three perpendicular axes. There is no limit on the difference between individual forward deformation readings. There is no specification for return deformation.

[2] All coloured dots shall be reasonable in size and placement.

e. All tests for rebound, mass, size, deformation and durability shall be made in accordance with the Regulations described in the current edition of *ITF Approved Tennis Balls, Classified Surfaces & Recognised Courts*.

## CLASSIFICATION OF COURT PACE

The ITF test method used for determining the pace of a court surface is ITF CS 01/02 (ITF Court Pace Rating) as described in the ITF publication entitled "ITF guide to test methods for tennis court surfaces".

Court surfaces which have an ITF Court Pace Rating of 0 to 29 shall be classified as being Category 1 (slow pace). Examples of court surface types which conform to this classification will include most clay courts and other types of unbound mineral surface.

Court surfaces which have an ITF Court Pace Rating of 30 to 34 shall be classified as being Category 2 (medium-slow pace), while court surfaces with an ITF Court Pace Rating of 35 to 39 shall be classified as being Category 3 (medium pace). Examples of court surface types which conform to this classification will include most acrylic coated surfaces plus some carpet surfaces.

Court surfaces with an ITF Court Pace Rating of 40 to 44 shall be classified as being Category 4 (medium-fast pace), while court surfaces which have an ITF Court Pace Rating of 45 or more shall be classified as being Category 5 (fast pace). Examples of court surface types which conform to this classification will include most natural grass, artificial grass and some carpet surfaces.

*Case 1: Which ball type should be used on which court surface?*

*Decision: 3 different types of balls are approved for play under the Rules of Tennis, however:*

a. *Ball Type 1 (fast speed) is intended for play on slow pace court surfaces.*

b. *Ball Type 2 (medium speed) is intended for play on medium-slow, medium and medium-fast pace court surfaces.*

c. *Ball Type 3 (slow speed) is intended for play on fast pace court surfaces.*

*Note:*

In addition to the ball types specified under paragraph (b) above, the Stage 1 (Green) ball may be used for all levels of competitive play except for world ranking professional tennis events, Davis Cup and Billie Jean King Cup, the Olympic and Paralympic Tennis Events, World Tennis Tour Men's, Women's and Junior Tournaments and Team events sanctioned by the ITF and affiliated Regional Associations, ITF Senior Circuit and Team events and ITF Wheelchair Tennis Tour Circuit and Team events.

Each National Association shall have the right to decide which national competitive events should use the Stage 1 (Green) ball.

# APPENDIX Ⅱ THE RACKET

For all measurements in Appendix II, SI units shall take precedence.

a. The racket shall consist of a frame and string(s). The frame shall consist of a handle and head, and may also include a throat. The head is defined as that part of the racket to which the string(s) connect. The handle is defined as that part of the racket connected to the head which is held by the player in normal use. The throat, where present, is that part of the racket that joins the handle to the head.

b. The hitting surface, defined as the main area of the stringing pattern bordered by the points of entry of the strings into the head or points of contact of the strings with the head, whichever is the smaller, shall be flat and consist of a pattern of crossed strings, which shall be alternately interlaced or bonded where they cross. The stringing pattern must be generally uniform and, in particular, not less dense in the centre than in any other area. The racket shall be designed and strung such that the playing characteristics are identical on both faces.

c. The racket shall not exceed 73.7 cm (29.0 inches) in overall length, and 31.7 cm (12.5 inches) in overall width. The hitting surface shall not exceed 39.4 cm (15.5 inches) in overall length, when measured parallel to the longitudinal axis of the handle, and 29.2 cm (11.5 inches) in overall width, when measured perpendicular to the longitudinal axis of the handle.

d. The racket shall be free of any attached object, protrusion or device which makes it possible to change materially the shape of the racket, or its moment of inertia about any principal axis, or to change any physical property which may affect the performance of the racket during the playing of a point. Attached objects, protrusions and devices that are approved as Player Analysis Technology, or that are utilised to limit or prevent wear and tear or vibration or, for the frame only, to distribute weight, are permitted. All permissible objects, protrusions and devices must be reasonable in size and placement for their respective purpose(s).

No energy source that in any way could change or affect the playing characteristics of a racket may be built into or attached to a racket.

# APPENDIX Ⅲ PLAYER ANALYSIS TECHNOLOGY

Player Analysis Technology is equipment that may perform any of the following functions with respect to player performance information:

a. Recording.

b. Storing.

c. Transmission.

d. Analysis.

e. Communication to a player of any kind and by any means.

Player Analysis Technology may record and/or store information during a match. Such information may only be accessed by a player in accordance with Rule 30.

# APPENDIX Ⅳ ADVERTISING

1. Advertising is permitted on the net as long as it is placed on the part of the net that is within 3 feet (0.914 m) from the centre of the net posts and is produced in such a way that it does not interfere with the vision of the players or the playing conditions. A mark (non-commercial) of the sanctioning body is permitted on the lower part of the net, minimum 20 inches (0.51 m) from the top of the net, as long as it is produced in such a way that it does not interfere with the vision of the players or the playing conditions.
2. Advertising and other marks or material placed at the back and sides of the court shall be permitted unless it interferes with the vision of the players or the playing conditions.
3. Advertising and other marks or material placed on the court surface outside the lines is permitted unless it interferes with the vision of the players or the playing conditions.
4. Notwithstanding paragraphs (1), (2) and (3) above, any advertising, marks or material placed on the net or placed at the back and sides of the court, or on the court surface outside the lines may not contain white or yellow or other light colours that may interfere with the vision of the players or the playing conditions.

5. Advertising and other marks or material are not permitted on the court surface inside the lines of the court.

# APPENDIX V ALTERNATIVE PROCEDURES AND SCORING METHODS

The alternatives listed in this Appendix V may be used.

## SCORE IN A GAME (Rule 5):

### "NO-AD" SCORING METHOD

A "No-Ad" game is scored as follows with the server's score being called first:

| | | |
|---|---|---|
| No points | - | "Love" |
| First point | - | "15" |
| Second point | - | "30" |
| Third point | - | "40" |
| Fourth point | - | "Game" |

If each player/team has won three points, the score is "Deuce" and a deciding point shall be played. The receiver(s) shall choose whether to receive the service from the right half or the left half of the court. In doubles, the players of the receiving team cannot change positions to receive this deciding point. The player/team who wins the deciding point wins the "Game".

In mixed doubles, the player of the same gender as the server shall receive the deciding point. The players of the receiving team cannot change positions to receive the deciding point.

## SCORE IN A SET (Rules 6 and 7):

1. SHORT SETS

The first player/team who wins four games wins that set, provided there is a margin of two games over the opponent(s). If the score reaches four games all, a tie-break game shall be played. Alternatively (at the discretion of the sanctioning body), if the score reaches three games all, a tie-break game shall be played.

2. SHORT SET TIE-BREAK

When playing Short Sets only, a Short Set tie-break may be used. The first player/team to win five points wins the "Game" and "Set", with a deciding point if the score reaches four all. The order and number of serves shall be determined by the sanctioning body. Players/Teams will only change ends after the first four points have been played.

3. MATCH TIE-BREAK (7 POINTS)

When the score in a match is one set all, or two sets all in best of five sets matches, one tie-break game shall be played to decide the match. This tie-break game replaces the deciding final set.

The player/team who first wins seven points shall win this match tie-break and the match provided there is a margin of two points over the opponent(s).

4. MATCH TIE-BREAK (10 POINTS)

When the score in a match is one set all, or two sets all in best of five sets matches, one tie-break game shall be played to decide the match. This tie-break game replaces the deciding final set. The player/team who first wins ten points shall win this match tie-break and the match provided there is a margin of two points over the opponent(s).

Note: *When using the match tie-break to replace the final set:*

- *the original order of service continues (Rules 5 and 14).*
- *in doubles, the order of serving and receiving within the team may be altered, as in the beginning of each set (Rules 14 and 15).*
- *before the start of the match tie-break there shall be a 120 seconds set break.*
- *balls should not be changed before the start of the match tie-break even if a ball change is due.*

## CHANGE OF ENDS (Rule 10):

During a tie-break game, players shall change ends after the first point and thereafter after every four points.

## THE LET DURING A SERVICE (Rule 22):

"NO LET" RULE

This alternative is play without the service let in Rule 22.a, whereby a serve that touches the net, strap or band is in play. At the discretion of the sanctioning body, when playing doubles using Short Sets in combination with No-Ad scoring and the No-Let rule, either player on the receiving team is permitted to return a serve that touches the net, strap or band and lands within the correct service box.

# APPENDIX Ⅵ ROLE OF COURT OFFICIALS

The referee is the final authority on all questions of tennis law and the referee's decision is final.

In matches where a chair umpire is assigned, the chair umpire is the final authority on all questions of fact during the match.

The players have the right to call the referee to court if they disagree with a chair umpire's interpretation of tennis law.

In matches where line umpires and net umpires are assigned, they make all calls (including foot-fault calls) relating to that line or net. The chair umpire has the right to overrule a line umpire or a net umpire if the chair umpire is sure that a clear mistake has been made. The chair umpire is responsible for calling any line (including foot-faults) or net where no line umpire or net umpire is assigned.

A line umpire who cannot make a call shall signal this immediately to the chair umpire who shall make a decision. If the line umpire can not make a call, or if there is no line umpire, and the chair umpire can not make a decision on a question of fact, the point shall be replayed.

In team events where the referee is sitting on-court, the referee is also the final authority on questions of fact.

Play may be stopped or suspended at any time the chair umpire decides it is necessary or appropriate.

The referee may also stop or suspend play in the case of darkness, weather or adverse court conditions. When play is suspended for darkness, this should be done at the end of a set, or after an even number of games have been played in the set in progress. After a suspension in play, the score and position of players on-court in the match shall stand when the match resumes.

The chair umpire or referee shall make decisions regarding continuous play and coaching in respect of any Code of Conduct that is approved and in operation.

Case 1: *The chair umpire awards the server a first service after an overrule, but the receiver argues that it should be a second service, since the server had already served a fault. Should the referee be called to court to give a decision?*

Decision: *Yes. The chair umpire makes the first decision about questions of tennis law (issues relating to the application of specific facts). However, if a player appeals the chair umpire's decision, then the referee shall be called to make the final decision.*

Case 2: *A ball is called "out", but a player claims that the ball was good. May the referee be called to court to make a decision?*

Decision: *No. The chair umpire makes the final decision on questions of fact (issues relating to what actually happened during a specific incident).*

Case 3: *Is a chair umpire allowed to overrule a line umpire at the end of a point if, in the chair umpire's opinion, a clear mistake was made earlier in the point?*

*Decision:* No. A chair umpire may only overrule a line umpire immediately after the clear mistake has been made.

*Case 4:* A line umpire calls a ball "Out" and then the player argues that the ball was good. Is the chair umpire allowed to overrule the line umpire?

*Decision:* No. A chair umpire must never overrule as the result of the protest or appeal by a player.

*Case 5:* A line umpire calls a ball "Out". The chair umpire was unable to see clearly, but thought the ball was in. May the chair umpire overrule the line umpire?

*Decision:* No. The chair umpire may only overrule when sure that the line umpire made a clear mistake.

*Case 6:* Is a line umpire allowed to change the call after the chair umpire has announced the score?

*Decision:* Yes. If a line umpire realises a mistake, a correction should be made as soon as possible provided it is not as the result of a protest or appeal of a player.

*Case 7:* If a chair umpire or line umpire calls "Out" and then corrects the call to good, what is the correct decision?

*Decision:* The chair umpire must decide if the original "Out" call was a hindrance to either player. If it was a hindrance, the point shall be replayed. If it was not a hindrance, the player who hit the ball wins the point.

*Case 8:* A ball is blown back over the net and the player correctly reaches over the net to try to play the ball. The opponent(s) hinders *the player from doing this. What is the correct decision?*

*Decision: The chair umpire must decide if the hindrance was deliberate or unintentional and either awards the point to the hindered player or order the point to be replayed.*

## BALL MARK INSPECTION PROCEDURES

1. Ball mark inspections can only be made on clay courts.
2. A ball mark inspection requested by a player (team) shall be allowed only if the chair umpire cannot determine the call with certainty from their chair on either a point-ending shot or when a player (team) stops playing the point during a rally (returns are permitted but then the player must immediately stop).
3. When the chair umpire has decided to make a ball mark inspection, they should go down from the chair and make the inspection themselves. If they do not know where the mark is, they can ask the line umpire for help in locating the mark, but then the chair umpire shall inspect it.
4. The original call or overrule will always stand if the line umpire and chair umpire cannot determine the location of the mark or if the mark is unreadable.
5. Once the chair umpire has identified and ruled on a ball mark, this decision is final and not appealable.
6. In clay court tennis the chair umpire should not be too quick to announce the score unless absolutely certain of the call. If in doubt, wait before calling the score to determine whether a ball mark inspection is necessary.
7. In doubles the appealing player must make their appeal in such a way that either play stops or the chair umpire stops play.

If an appeal is made to the chair umpire, then they must first determine that the correct appeal procedure was followed. If it was not correct or if it was late, then the chair umpire may determine that the opposing team was deliberately hindered.

8. If a player erases the ball mark before the chair umpire has made a final decision, they concede the call.
9. A player may not cross the net to check a ball mark without being subject to the Unsportsmanlike Provision of the Code of Conduct.

## ELECTRONIC REVIEW PROCEDURES

At tournaments where an Electronic Review System is used, the following procedures should be followed for matches on courts where it is used.

1. A request for an Electronic Review of a line call or overrule by a player (team) shall be allowed only on either a point-ending shot or when a player (team) stops playing the point during a rally (returns are permitted but then the player must immediately stop).
2. The chair umpire should decide to use the Electronic Review when there is doubt about the accuracy of the line call or overrule. However, the chair umpire may refuse the Electronic Review if they believe that the player is making an unreasonable request or that it was not made in a timely manner.
3. In doubles the appealing player must make their appeal in such a way that either play stops or the chair umpire stops play. If an appeal is made to the chair umpire, then they must first determine that the correct appeal procedure was followed. If it was not correct or if it was late, then the chair umpire may determine that the opposing team was deliberately hindered, in which case the appealing team loses the point.
4. The original call or overrule will always stand if the Electronic Review is unable, for whatever reason, to make a decision on

that line call or overrule.

5. The chair umpire's final decision will be the outcome of the Electronic Review and is not appealable. If a manual choice is required for the system to review a particular ball impact, a review official approved by the referee shall decide which ball impact is reviewed.

6. Each player (team) is allowed three (3) unsuccessful appeals per set, plus one (1) additional appeal in the tie-break. For matches with advantage sets, players (teams) will start again with a maximum of three (3) unsuccessful appeals at 6 games all and every 12 games thereafter. For matches with match tie-break, the match tie-break counts as a new set and each player (team) starts with three (3) appeals. Players (teams) will have an unlimited number of successful appeals.

# APPENDIX Ⅶ 10 AND UNDER TENNIS COMPETITION

## Courts:

In addition to the (full sized) court described in Rule 1, the following court dimensions may be used for 10 and under tennis competition:

- A court, designated "Red" for the purposes of 10 and under tennis competition, shall be a rectangle, between 36 feet (10.97 m) and 42 feet (12.80 m) long, and between 14 feet (4.27 m) and 20 feet (6.10 m) wide. The net shall be between 31.5 inches (0.800 m) and 33.0 inches (0.838 m) high at the centre.
- A court, designated "Orange", shall be a rectangle, between 58 feet (17.68 m) and 60 feet (18.29 m) long, and between 20 feet (6.10 m) and 27 feet (8.23 m) wide. The net shall be between 31.5 inches (0.800 m) and 36.0 inches (0.914 m) high at the centre.

## Balls:

Only the following ball types, which are specified in Appendix I, can be used in 10 and under tennis competition:

- A Stage 3 (Red) ball, which is recommended for play on a "red" court, by players aged up to 8 years, using a racket up to 23 inches (58.4 cm) long.

- A Stage 2 (Orange) ball, which is recommended for play on an "orange" court, by players aged 8 to 10 years, using a racket between 23 inches (58.4 cm) and 25 inches (63.5 cm) long.
- A Stage 1 (Green) ball, which is recommended for play on a full size court, by advanced players aged 9 to 10 years, using a racket between 25 inches (63.5 cm) and 26 inches (66.0 cm) long.

*Note: Other ball types described in Appendix I cannot be used in 10 and under tennis competition.*

## Scoring methods:

For 10 and under tennis competition using Stage 3 (Red), Stage 2 (Orange) or Stage 1 (Green) balls, scoring methods specified in the Rules of Tennis (including those specified in Appendix V) can be utilised, in addition to short duration scoring methods involving matches of one match tie-break, best of 3 tie-breaks/match tie-breaks, one short set or one regular set.

## Timed matches:

For 10 and under tennis competition the tournament committee may set a specific time period for matches in the event.

# APPENDIX Ⅷ PLAN OF THE COURT

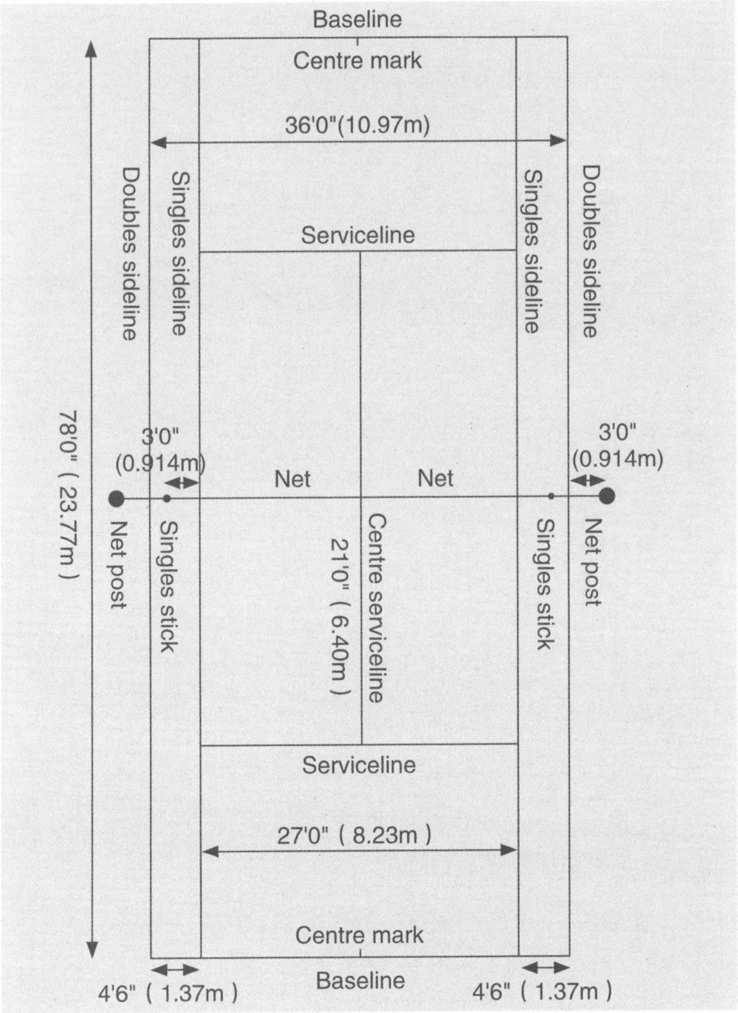


Note: *All court measurements shall be made to the outside of the lines.*

# APPENDIX Ⅸ SUGGESTIONS ON HOW TO MARK OUT A COURT

## Including Blended Lines

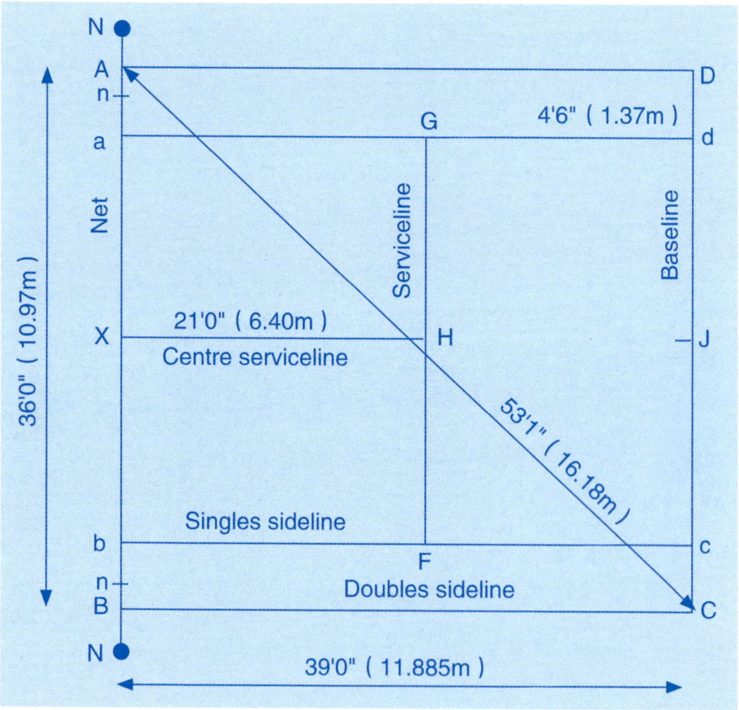


*Note: All court measurements shall be made to the outside of the lines.*

The following procedure is for the usual combined doubles and singles court (See note at foot for a court for one purpose only).

First select the position of the net; a straight line 42 feet (12.80 m) long. Mark the centre (X on the diagram above) and, measuring from there in each direction, mark:

at 13'6" (4.11 m) the points a, b, where the net crosses the inner sidelines, at 16'6" (5.03 m) the positions of the singles sticks (n, n), at 18'0" (5.48 m) the points A, B, where the net crosses the outer sidelines, at 21'0" (6.40 m) the positions of the net posts (N, N), being the ends of the original 42'0" (12.80 m) line.

Insert pegs at A and B and attach to them the respective ends of two measuring tapes. On one, which will measure the diagonal of the half-court, take a length 53'1"(16.18 m) and on the other (to measure the sideline) a length of 39'0" (11.89 m). Pull both taut so that at these distances they meet at a point C, which is one corner of the court. Reverse the measurements to find the other corner D.

As a check on this operation it is advisable at this stage to verify the length of the line CD which, being the baseline, should be found to be 36'0" (10.97 m); and at the same time its centre J can be marked, and also the ends of the inner sidelines (c, d), 4'6" (1.37 m) from C and D.

The centreline and serviceline are now marked by means of the points F, H, G, which are measured 21'0" (6.40 m) from the net down the lines bc, XJ, ad, respectively.

Identical procedure the other side of the net completes the court.

If a singles court only is required, no lines are necessary outside the points a, b, c, d, but the court can be measured out as above. Alternatively, the corners of the baseline (c, d) can be found if preferred by pegging the two tapes at a and b instead of at A and B, and by then using lengths of 47'5" (14.46 m) and 39'0" (11.89 m). The net posts will be at n, n, and a 33'0" (10 m) singles net should be used.

When a combined doubles and singles court with a doubles net is used for singles, the net must be supported at the points n, n, to a height of 3 feet 6 inches (1.07 m) by means of two singles sticks, which shall be not more than 3 inches (7.5 cm) square or 3 inches (7.5 cm) in diameter. The centres of the singles sticks shall be 3 feet (0.914 m) outside the singles court on each side.

To assist in the placing of these singles sticks it is desirable that the points n, n, should each be shown with a white dot when the court is marked.

When sanctioning bodies approve so called "Blended Lines" on courts the following guidelines must be followed:

Colour:

- Within the same colour family as the background playing surface.
- Lighter than the background playing surface.
- Limit on colour variation of +22 points on the L* scale(Add ≤25% by volume of white paint to the background colour).

Pace:

• Within 5 CPR of the playing surface.

Dimensions:

• 1.0-1.5 cm narrower than the standard lines.

Marking:

• Terminate 8 cm from intersection with white playing lines.

*Note:*

*As a guide for international competitions, the recommended minimum distance between the baselines and the backstops should be 21 feet (6.40 m) and between the sidelines and the sidestops the recommended minimum distance should be 12 feet (3.66 m).*

*As a guide for recreational and Club play, the recommended minimum distance between the baselines and the backstops should be 18 feet (5.48 m) and between the sidelines and the sidestops the recommended minimum distance should be 10 feet (3.05 m).*

*As a guide, the recommended minimum height measured at the net from the court surface to the ceiling should be 29.6 feet (9.0 m).*

## APPENDIX X RULES OF BEACH TENNIS

The Rules of Beach Tennis are approved by the Rules of Tennis Committee and the Board of Directors and can be found on https://www.itftennis.com/en/itf-tours/beach-tennis-tour/

# APPENDIX XI PROCEDURES FOR REVIEW AND HEARINGS ON THE RULES OF TENNIS

## 1. INTRODUCTION

1.1 These procedures were approved by the Board of Directors of the International Tennis Federation ("Board of Directors") on 17 May 1998.

1.2 The Board of Directors may from time to time supplement, amend, or vary these procedures.

## 2. OBJECTIVES

2.1 The International Tennis Federation is the custodian of the Rules of Tennis and is committed to:

a. Preserving the traditional character and integrity of the game of tennis.

b. Actively preserving the skills traditionally required to play the game.

c. Encouraging improvements, which maintain the challenge of the game.

d. Ensuring fair competition.

2.2 To ensure fair, consistent and expeditious review and hearings in relation to the Rules of Tennis the procedures set out below shall apply.

## 3. SCOPE

These Procedures shall apply to Rulings under:

a. Rule 1 – The Court.

b. Rule 3 – The Ball.

c. Rule 4 – The Racket.

d. Appendix I and II of the Rules of Tennis.

e. Any other Rules of Tennis which the International Tennis Federation may decide.

## 4. STRUCTURE

4.1 Under these procedures Rulings shall be issued by a Ruling Board.

4.2 Such Rulings shall be final save, for an entitlement to appeal to an Appeal Tribunal pursuant to these procedures.

## 5. APPLICATION

Rulings shall be taken either:

a. Following a motion of the Board of Directors; or

b. Upon the receipt of an application in accordance with the procedures set out below.

## 6. APPOINTMENT AND COMPOSITION OF RULING BOARDS

6.1 Ruling Boards shall be appointed by the President of the International Tennis Federation ("President") or their designee and shall comprise of such a number, as the President or their designee shall determine.

6.2 If more than one person is appointed to the Ruling Board the Ruling Board shall nominate one person from amongst themselves to act as Chairperson.

6.3 The Chairperson shall be entitled to regulate the procedures prior to and at any review and/or hearing of a Ruling Board.

## 7. PROPOSED RULINGS BY THE RULING BOARD

7.1 The details of any proposed Ruling issued upon the motion of the Board of Directors may be provided to any bona fide person or any players, equipment manufacturer or national association or members thereof with an interest in the proposed Ruling.

7.2 Any person so notified shall be given a reasonable period within which to forward comments, objections, or requests for information to the President or his designee in connection with the proposed Ruling.

## 8. APPLICATION FOR RULINGS

8.1 An application for a Ruling may be made by any party with a bona fide interest in the Ruling including any player, equipment manufacturer or national association or member thereof.

8.2 Any application for a Ruling must be submitted in writing to the President.

8.3 To be valid an application for a Ruling must include the following minimum information:

a. The full name and address of the Applicant.

b. The date of the application.

c. A statement clearly identifying the interest of the Applicant in the question upon which a Ruling is requested.

d. All relevant documentary evidence upon which the Applicant intends to rely at any hearing.

e. If, in the opinion of the Applicant, expert evidence is necessary they shall include a request for such expert evidence to be heard. Such request must identify the name of any expert proposed and their relevant expertise.

f. When an application for a Ruling on a racket or other piece of equipment is made, a prototype or, exact, copy of the equipment in question must be submitted with the application for a Ruling.

g. If, in the opinion of the Applicant, there are extraordinary or unusual circumstances, which require a Ruling to be made within a specified time or before a specified date they shall include a statement describing the extraordinary or unusual circumstances.

8.4 If an application for a Ruling does not contain the information and/or equipment referred to at Clause 8.3 (a)-(g) above the President or their designee shall notify the Applicant giving the Applicant a specified reasonable time within which to remedy the defect. If the Applicant fails to remedy the defect within the specified time the application shall be dismissed.

## 9. CONVENING THE RULING BOARD

9.1 On receipt of a valid application or on the motion of the Board of Directors the President or their designee may convene a Ruling Board to deal with the application or motion.

9.2 The Ruling Board need not hold a hearing to deal with an application or motion where the application or motion, in the opinion of the Chairperson can be resolved in a fair manner without a hearing.

## 10. PROCEDURE OF THE RULING BOARD

10.1 The Chairperson of a Ruling Board shall determine the appropriate form, procedure and date of any review and/or hearing.

10.2 The Chairperson shall provide written notice of those matters set out at 10.1 above to any Applicant or any person or association who has expressed an interest in the proposed Ruling.

10.3 The Chairperson shall determine all matters relating to evidence and shall not be bound by judicial rules governing procedure and admissibility of evidence provided that the review and/or hearing is conducted in a fair manner with a reasonable opportunity for the relevant parties to present their case.

10.4 Under these procedures any review and/or hearings:

a. Shall take place in private.

b. May be adjourned and/or postponed by the Ruling Board.

10.5 The Chairperson shall have the discretion to co-opt from time to time additional members onto the Ruling Board with special skill or experience to deal with specific issues, which require such special skill or experience.

10.6 The Ruling Board shall take its decision by a simple majority. No member of the Ruling Board may abstain.

10.7 The Chairperson shall have the complete discretion to make such order against the Applicant [and/or other individuals or organisations commenting objecting or requesting information at any review and/or hearing] in relation to the costs of the application and/or the reasonable expenses incurred by the Ruling Board in holding tests or obtaining reports relating to equipment subject to a Ruling as he shall deem appropriate.

## 11. NOTIFICATION

11.1 Once a Ruling Board has reached a decision it shall provide written notice to the Applicant, or any person or association who has expressed an interest in the proposed Ruling as soon as reasonably practicable.

11.2 Such written notice shall include a summary of the reasoning behind the decision of the Ruling Board.

11.3 Upon notification to the Applicant or upon such other date specified by the Ruling Board the Ruling of the Ruling Board shall be immediately binding under the Rules of Tennis.

## 12. APPLICATION OF CURRENT RULES OF TENNIS

12.1 Subject to the power of the Ruling Board to issue interim Rulings the current Rules of Tennis shall continue to apply until any review and/or hearing of the Ruling Board is concluded and a Ruling issued by the Ruling Board.

12.2 Prior to and during any review and/or hearing the Chairperson of the Ruling Board may issue such directions as are deemed reasonably necessary in the implementation of the Rules of Tennis and of these procedures including the issue of interim Rulings.

12.3 Such interim Rulings may include restraining orders on the use of any equipment under the Rules of Tennis pending a Ruling by the Ruling Board as to whether or not the equipment meets the specification of the Rules of Tennis.

## 13. APPOINTMENT AND COMPOSITION OF APPEAL TRIBUNALS

13.1 Appeal Tribunals shall be appointed by the President or his designee from members of the Board of Directors.

13.2 No member of the Ruling Board who made the original Ruling shall be a member of the Appeal Tribunal.

13.3 The Appeal Tribunal shall comprise of such number as the President or their designee shall determine but shall be no less than three.

13.4 The Appeal Tribunal shall nominate one person from amongst themselves to act as Chairperson.

13.5 The Chairperson shall be entitled to regulate the procedures prior to and at any appeal hearing.

## 14. APPLICATION TO APPEAL

14.1 An Applicant [or a person or association who has expressed an interest and forwarded any comments, objections, or requests to a proposed Ruling] may appeal any Ruling of the Ruling Board.

14.2 To be valid an application for an appeal must be:

a. Made in writing to the Chairperson of the Ruling Board who made the Ruling appealed not later than 45 days following notification of the Ruling;

b. Must set out details of the Ruling appealed against; and

c. Must contain the full grounds of the appeal.

14.3 Upon receipt of a valid application to appeal the Chairperson of the Ruling Board making the original Ruling may require a reasonable appeal fee to be paid by the Appellant as a condition of appeal. Such appeal fee shall be repaid to the

Appellant if the appeal is successful.

## 15. CONVENING THE APPEAL TRIBUNAL

15.1 The President or their designee shall convene the Appeal Tribunal following payment by the Appellant of any appeal fee.

## 16. PROCEDURES OF APPEAL TRIBUNAL

16.1 The Appeal Tribunal and their Chairperson shall conduct procedures and hearings in accordance with those matters set out in sections 10, 11 and 12 above.

16.2 Upon notification to the Appellant or upon such other date specified by the Appeal Tribunal the Ruling of the Appeal Tribunal shall be immediately binding and final under the Rules of Tennis.

## 17. GENERAL

17.1 If a Ruling Board consists of only one member that single member shall be responsible for regulating the hearing as Chairperson and shall determine the procedures to be followed prior to and during any review and/or hearing.

17.2 All review and/or hearings shall be conducted in English. In any hearing where an Applicant, and/or other individuals or organisations commenting, objecting or requesting information do not speak English an interpreter must be present. Wherever practicable the interpreter shall be independent.

17.3 The Ruling Board or Appeal Tribunal may publish extracts from its own Rulings.

17.4 All notifications to be made pursuant to these procedures shall be in writing.

17.5 Any notifications made pursuant to these procedures shall be deemed notified upon the date that they were communicated, sent or transmitted to the Applicant or other relevant party.

17.6 A Ruling Board shall have the discretion to dismiss an application if in its reasonable opinion the application is substantially similar to an application or motion upon which a Ruling Board has made a decision and/or Ruling within the 36 months prior to the date of the application.

# 2023 VARIATIONS TO THE RULES

To enable trials to be conducted on potential changes to the Rules of Tennis, applications may be made by interested parties for variations to the Rules for a limited duration and/or limited events. Applications are considered by the Rules of Tennis Committee, which, if approved, are submitted to the ITF Board of Directors for ratification.

The following temporary variations to the Rules of Tennis were originally granted by the ITF Board of Directors for 2020, 2021 and 2022, but due to the limited number of events held during 2021 arising from the Covid-19 pandemic, and following consultation with the applicants, the variations have been extended to the 2023 Rules.

## Rule 2—Permanent Fixtures:

- Companies that have obtained ITF Approval for Player Analysis Technology (PAT) equipment may attach those PAT devices to the tennis net post(s), to enable line-calling and player analytics.

## Rule 30—Coaching:

- The WTA, ATP and Grand Slams may conduct trials of off-court coaching at their events.

## Appendix Ⅴ—Alternative procedures and scoring methods:

- The Grand Slams may conduct a trial of a 10-point tie-break when the score reaches 6-6 in the final set of men's and women's singles and doubles draws, including wheelchair singles and doubles matches and juniors singles matches, during their events.

## Rules of Beach Tennis, Appendix III—The Ball:

- Beach Tennis tournaments may use Stage 2 tennis balls in alternative colours to those specified in the Rules (e.g. blue and yellow, purple and yellow, purple and orange, purple and green).

## Appendix Ⅶ—10 and under Tennis Competition:

- The following net heights may be used for 10 and under tennis competition:
  - For a court designated "red", a net height of between 23.6 inches (0.600 m) and 25.6 inches (0.650 m) high at the centre.

- For a court designated "orange", a net height of between 25.6 inches (0.650 m) and 27.6 inches (0.700 m) high at the centre.
- For a court designated "green", i.e. the (full size) court described in Rule 1, a net height of between 27.6 inches (0.700 m) and 31.5 inches (0.800 m) high at the centre.

During this trial period, each National Association shall have the right to decide on the height of the net at the centre, limited to the options given above, for each of the three stages for 10 and under competition.

Upon the conclusion of each trial, the applicant shall provide a report to the Rules of Tennis Committee.

The Rules of Tennis Committee is comprised of representatives of the Grand Slams, ATP, WTA and ITF National Tennis Associations.